符号中国 SIGNS OF CHINA

长江黄河

THE YANGTZE RIVER AND THE YELLOW RIVER

"符号中国"编写组 ◎ 编著

中央民族大学出版社
China Minzu University Press

图书在版编目(CIP)数据

长江黄河：汉文、英文 /"符号中国"编写组编著. — 北京：
中央民族大学出版社, 2024.8
（符号中国）
ISBN 978-7-5660-2355-1

Ⅰ.①长… Ⅱ.①符… Ⅲ.①长江—介绍—汉、英 ②黄河—介绍—汉、英
Ⅳ.①K928.42

中国国家版本馆CIP数据核字（2024）第016993号

符号中国：长江黄河 THE YANGTZE RIVER AND THE YELLOW RIVER

编　　著	"符号中国"编写组
策划编辑	沙　平
责任编辑	黄修义
英文指导	李瑞清
英文编辑	邱　械
美术编辑	曹　娜　郑亚超　洪　涛
出版发行	中央民族大学出版社
	北京市海淀区中关村南大街27号　邮编：100081
	电话：（010）68472815（发行部）　传真：（010）68933757（发行部）
	（010）68932218（总编室）　　　　（010）68932447（办公室）
经 销 者	全国各地新华书店
印 刷 厂	北京兴星伟业印刷有限公司
开　　本	787 mm×1092 mm 1/16　印张：9.75
字　　数	135千字
版　　次	2024年8月第1版　2024年8月第1次印刷
书　　号	ISBN 978-7-5660-2355-1
定　　价	58.00元

版权所有　侵权必究

"符号中国"丛书编委会

唐兰东　巴哈提　杨国华　孟靖朝　赵秀琴

本册编写者

马利琴

前言 Preface

　　世界上著名的文明古国大都起源于大河流域，而古老的中华民族就是在长江和黄河两岸孕育发展起来的。长江和黄河都发源自"世界屋脊"——青藏高原，一路奔腾向前，流过崇山峻岭、平原丘陵，向东流入

All the world-famous ancient civilizations originate from the large river basins. Without exception, the ancient Chinese nation is bred by the Yangtze River and the Yellow River. Both the two rivers originate from the "spine of the world"—Qinghai-Xizang Plateau and surge forward, flow through high mountains,

大海。长江与黄河的中下游地区是中华民族开发最早的地区，早在数万年前中华民族祖先就在横贯东西、沟通南北的两大江河边繁衍生息，不断创造和发展着中华文明。长江文化与黄河文化的来源与发展各不相同，因而有着各自不同的文化特色。但在几千年的发展历程中，两大文化系统经过不断地交流和融合，成为中国传统文化最重要的组成部分。本书着眼于长江、黄河文化对中华民族五千年文明的推动作用，详细介绍了长江与黄河的起源与分段、支流与湖泊、文明遗迹以及两岸名城，希望读者通过本书对长江与黄河能有更为切近、深入、全面的认识。

plains and lofty hills, at last enter into the sea. The middle and lower reaches areas of the Yangtze River and the Yellow River are the earliest regions developed by the Chinese nation. The Chinese ancestors had been settled by the two rivers as early as tens of thousands years ago and continuously creating and developing the Chinese civilization. The origins and developments of the Yangtze River and the Yellow River cultures are different and distinct in cultural characteristics. But during the development history of thousands years, the two cultural systems kept communicating and fusing and became the most important components of traditional Chinese culture. This book focuses on the Yangtze River and the Yellow River cultures' promoting effect on the five thousand years of civilization of the Chinese nation, and introduces the headstreams, sections, tributaries, lakes, historical sites and major cities of the Yangtze River and the Yellow River in detail. Wish the readers have a more detailed, intensive and comprehensive knowledge of the two rivers after reading this book.

目 录 Contents

亚洲第一大河——长江
The Yangtze River— Longest River of Asia..... 001

长江的源流
Origin of the Yangtze River............................. 002

长江文明
The Yangtze River Civilization......................... 027

长江两岸名城
Major Cities by the Yangtze River....................040

中华民族的母亲河——黄河
The Yellow River—Mother River of Chinese Nation 077

黄河的源流
Origin of the Yellow River 078

黄河文明
The Yellow River Civilization 105

黄河两岸名城
Major Cities by the Yellow River 115

亚洲第一大河——长江
The Yangtze River—Longest River of Asia

　　长江，身在中国境内，是世界第三大流量的河流，仅次于亚马孙河和刚果河。

　　长江，全长6300千米，仅次于尼罗河和亚马孙河，是世界第三长河。

　　长江，是亚洲第一大河、世界第三大河，也是世界上最长的完全在一个国家境内的河流。

The Yangtze River is located within the territory of China. The quantity of flow of the Yangtze River ranks number three in the world, just next to the Amazon River and the Congo River.

　　6300 kilometers overall length makes the Yangtze River be the world's third longest river next to the River Nile and the Amazon River.

　　The Yangtze River is the longest river in Asia and the third longest river in the world. Meanwhile, it's the longest river completely flowing within a single country.

> 长江的源流

长江从青藏高原出发，向东流经青海、四川、西藏、云南、重庆、湖北、湖南、江西、安徽、江苏、上海等11个省、自治区、直辖市，最后注入东海。

长江源头

长江的源头位于世界屋脊——青藏高原的中心，位于号称"亚洲屋脊"的昆仑山脉和唐古拉山脉两大山脉之间。这里海拔在4500米以上，地势高耸，山体庞大，终年积雪。巍峨的雪山上冰川高悬，雪峰下沼泽遍布。每到冰雪融化的季节，一股股融水汇成许多水流。其中较大的河流有三条，即沱沱河、当曲和楚玛尔河。其中沱沱河最长，河道比其他两条顺直，人们根

> Origin of the Yangtze River

The Yangtze River starts from the Qinghai-Xizang Plateau, and flows through 11 provinces, autonomous regions and cities including Qinghai, Sichuan, Xizang, Yunnan, Chongqing, Hubei, Hunan, Jiangxi, Anhui, Jiangsu and Shanghai. At last, the river heads east and enters into the East China Sea.

Headstream of the Yangtze River

The headstream of the Yangtze River is located in the center area of the "spine of the world"—Qinghai-Xizang Plateau, between the "Asian Spine" Kunlun Mountains and the Tangula Mountains. The elevation of the headstream is over 4500 meters, where perennially snow-topped mountain peaks can be found everywhere. There are many swamps by the feet of the snow-capped mountains. When the season of ice and snow melting

- 沱沱河大桥边的"长江源"纪念碑（图片提供：全景正片）
Headstream of the Yangtze River Momument by the Tuotuo River Bridge

据"河源唯远"的原则，确定沱沱河为长江的正源。

沱沱河发源于唐古拉山脉主峰各拉丹冬雪山的西南侧，全长375千米，流域面积1.69万平方千米。各拉comes, the glaciers on the towering snow-capped mountains melt into many stream flows. Among which there are three major ones, the Tuotuo River, the Dangqu and the Qumar River. The longest of the three is the Tuotuo River, and its river channel

丹冬雪山与周围20余座雪山组成庞大的雪山群，山上晶莹夺目的积雪和冰川储存着大量的固体水源。冰川末端的冰舌融水沿冰崖泻下，形成一股股小瀑布，这就是长江的源头，波涛万里的长江就是从这里开始的。一条条的冰川融水汇流为沱沱河，穿过雪山谷地，流出唐古拉山区，继续北流，接纳了支流当曲之后，便称为"通天河"。

"当曲"在藏语中是"沼泽河"的意思，这里有世界上海拔最高的沼泽地，到处是连片的沼泽和泉群。从高空俯瞰，大大小小的水潭星罗棋布，在阳光下闪烁，十分壮观。

楚玛尔河发源于昆仑山南支的可可西里山的东部，形状像条狭长的带子。"楚玛尔"为藏语，意为"红水河"。楚玛尔河流过三江源地区的北部，上游河床宽浅、水流散乱、沙滩广布，多风积沙丘，水量较小，到下游接纳了昆仑山南坡丰富的冰雪融水和地下水之后，水量明显增大，汇入通天河，成为长江的一大水流来源。

is straighter than the other two. As a result, people define the Tuotuo River to be the headstream of the Yangtze River in accordance with the principle of "furthest source being the headstream".

The Tuotuo River originates from the southwestern side of the Geladandong Mountain, which is the main peak of the Tangula Mountains. It flows over a distance of 375 kilometers and drains an area of 16.9 thousand square kilometers. The Geladandong Mountain and the roughly 20 snow mountains aside constitute a large snow mountain group, on which the snow and glaciers reserve vast solid water. The bottom of the glaciers melt and the water flows down the glacial cliffs, many little waterfalls are formed. The giant Yangtze River is right originated from these tiny waterfalls. The streams of the melting water converge and constitute the Tuotuo River, which runs through the snow mountain valleys, flows out of the Tangula Mountains, and keeps heading north. It is called the Tongtian River after it combines the tributary Dangqu.

Dangqu means "river swamp" in Zang language. It is located in the swampland with the highest elevation in the world, where a good deal of swamps and springs spread. From a bird's-eye

三江源自然保护区

　　三江源自然保护区位于青藏高原腹地、青海省南部，为长江、黄河和澜沧江的源头汇水区。其西南与西藏接壤，东部与四川毗邻，总面积为36.6万平方公里。这里水资源丰富，河流纵横，湖泊众多，沼泽地分布广泛，还分布着大面积的现代冰川，是三条大河径流补给的主要源泉，因而被誉为"中国水塔"。作为中国面积最大、海拔最高的天然湿地，三江源地区具有独特而典型的高寒生态系统。这里地形地貌复杂，环境类型多样，也是世界上物种最丰富、最集中的地区之一。共有包括藏羚羊、野牦牛、藏原羚、喜马拉雅旱獭等在内的70余种青藏高原特有的珍稀物种在这里繁衍生息。

National Nature Reserve of Three Rivers Source

The National Nature Reserve of Three Rivers Source is located in south Qinghai Province, the central region of the Qinghai-Xizang Plateau. It's the source water catchment area of the Yangtze River, the Yellow River and the Lancang River. Northeast to Xizang and west to Sichuan, the total area of the reserve is 366 thousand square kilometers. The National Nature Reserve of Three Rivers Source is crowned as "the water-tower of China", with countless rivers, lakes, swampland, and extensive contemporary glaciers within the area. The rich water resources promote it as the key supply source of the three major rivers. As the natural wetland with the largest area and highest elevation in China, the Three Rivers Source Area possesses a unique and typical alpine ecosystem. The complex geomorphologies and multitudinous environmental forms provide the area with the most plentiful and centralized biodiversity in the world. Over 70 varieties of rare wild animals live here, including the endemic species of the Qinghai-Xizang Plateau like the Zang antelope, wild yak, goa and Himalayan marmot.

长江分段

　　按不同的水文、地貌特征，长江干流通常被划分为上游、中游、下游三段：从河源至湖北宜昌为上游段，宜昌至江西湖口为中游段，

view, pools of different sizes dot the landscape and glint in the sunshine. That scene is very spectacular.

　　The Qumar River originates from the eastern of the Hoh Xil Mountain, the southern branch of the Kunlun

穿行于群山峡谷之中的金沙江
Jinsha River Passing Through the Mountains and Gorges

Mountains, shapes like a long narrow belt. *Qumar* is from the Zang language and means "red river". The river flows through the northern Three Rivers Source Area. In its upper reaches, the riverbed is wide and shallow, the stream is scattered, the river is full of sandy beaches and sand dunes piled up by the winds, and the water volume is small. But in the lower reaches, after absorbing the plentiful snowmelt from the southern slope of the Kunlun Mountains and taking in the vast underground water, the water volume of the river increases significantly. After then it joins the Tongtian River and becomes one of the major water sources of the Yangtze River.

Sections of the Yangtze River

The main stream of the Yangtze River is divided into upper reaches, middle reaches and lower reaches in accordance with the different hydrology and geomorphology features. The upper reaches start from its headstream to Yichang in Hubei Province; the middle

湖口以下为下游段。

　　长江上游段长4529千米，约占总长度的72%。上游的沱沱河和通天河穿行于青藏高原腹地，河谷开阔，河槽宽浅，河道蜿蜒曲折，水流缓慢散乱，岔流很多。从四川省甘孜藏族自治州的巴塘河口到宜宾市这一段，古称"金沙江"，因地形突变、山高谷深，河流绝大部分穿行于峡谷之中，河水湍急。到云南石鼓以下，江水突然转向东北流，著名的虎跳峡就在石鼓以下，峡长16千米，最窄处仅30米。自宜宾以下至湖北宜昌之间的河段，习惯上称"川江"，河道蜿蜒于四川盆地之内，河床平缓，沿途接纳沱江、嘉陵江和乌江等众多支流，水量大增，江面变宽。过重庆奉节的白帝城，就进入了举世闻名的长江三峡（瞿塘峡、巫峡、西陵峡），长约193千米。

长江中游段从宜昌开始，长927千米。江水进入长江中下游平原，江面宽阔，水流缓慢，河道弯曲。其中，从湖北的枝城到湖南城陵矶一段，因古代属荆州地区，所以取名为"荆江"，素有"九曲回肠"之称。中游两岸湖泊众多，江湖相通，构成洞庭湖和鄱阳湖两大水系。

下游段水深江宽，从湖口到入海口共长844千米。江苏省扬州、镇江一带的长江干流又称"扬子

reaches are from Yichang to Hukou in Jiangxi Province; sections after Hukou refer to the lower reaches.

The length of the upper reaches is 4529 kilometers, accounting for about 72% of the overall length of the Yangtze River. The Tuotuo River and the Tongtian River in the upper reaches flow through the hinterland of the Qinghai-Xizang Plateau with broad river valleys, wide and shallow riverbed, wandering channel, slow and scattered water flow, and lots of branches. The section from the Batang estuary in Garze Zang Autonomous Prefecture to Yibin City has been called the Jinsha River since ancient times, where the topography is fickle, the mountains are high and the valleys are deep. Most of the river in this section flows fast through the gorges. When the river arrives at Shigu in Yunnan Province, the channel suddenly zigzags northeast. The famous Tiger Leaping Gorge is right near Shigu. The gorge is 16 kilometers long, and the narrowest place is only 30 meters. The section from Yibin to Yichang in Hubei Province is traditionally called the Chuanjiang River. The channel creeps into the Sichuan Basin and the river is mild. Meanwhile after absorbing several tributaries

- **云南德钦的金沙江大拐弯**

长江从青藏高原奔腾而下,进入云南境内后,与澜沧江、怒江一起在横断山脉的峡谷中穿行,形成"三江并流"的壮丽景观。到了云南香格里拉市的沙松碧村,突然转向东北,形成了罕见的"V"字形大弯,这个奇观被称为"长江第一湾"。

Great Bend of Jinsha River in Deqin in Yunnan Province

The Yangtze River rushing down the Qinghai-Xizang Plateau into Yunnan Province, passing through the gorges of the Hengduan Mountains together with the Lancang River and the Nujiang River, constitute the spectacular scene of the "Three Parallel Rivers". When arriving at Shasongbi village in Shangri-La City in Yunnan Province, the Yangtze River suddenly zigzags northeast, forming a uncommon "V" type bend, which is called the First Bend of the Yangtze River.

including the Tuojiang River, the Jialing River and the Wujiang River, the water volume of the river largely increases and the surface of the river is also widened. After passing Baidi Castle in Fengjie in Chongqing, the river flows to the world-famous Three Gorges (Qutang Gorge, Wuxia Gorge and Xiling Gorge), which is 193 kilometers long.

Passing the Three Gorges, the Yangtze River arrives at Yichang. Since then the river comes to its 927 kilometers long middle reaches and enters into the Yangtze Plain. The surface of the river is widened, the speed of water slows down and the channel is bended. Among the reaches, as the part from Zhicheng in Hubei Province to Chenglingji in Hunan Province belonged to the Jing area in ancient times, this section is called the "Jingjiang River", which has long been known as the "Bitter Zigzag". The plentiful interlinked lakes spread on the both banks of the Yangtze River's middle reaches constitute the 2 major water systems of the Dongting Lake and the Poyang Lake.

The lower reaches start from Hukou to the mouth of the Yangtze River, which is 844 kilometers long. In this section the water is deep and the river is wide.

• 《长江万里图》夏圭（宋）
Ten Thousand Miles Long Yangtze River by Xia Gui (Song Dynasty)

江",现在外国人常用"扬子江"这一名称泛指整个长江。由于海水倒灌,江水流速减缓,所携带的泥沙便在下游河段沉积下来,因此在江心形成了数十个大小不一的沙洲,其中最大的是崇明岛。

The main stream near Yangzhou and Zhenjiang in Jiangsu Province is specially called the "Yangtze River", which is now commonly used by foreigners to refer to the whole river in a general sense. Because of the sea water encroachment, the flow rate is slowed down. As a result, the silts carried by the river deposit in the lower reaches and form dozens of sandbars in uneven sizes in the middle of the river, among which the Chongming Island is the biggest one.

长江三峡

  长江三峡是长江中游的一段峡谷，西起重庆奉节县的白帝城，东至湖北宜昌市的南津关，由瞿塘峡、巫峡、西陵峡组成，全长193千米。三峡的形成是这一地区地壳不断上升，长江水强烈下切的结果。两岸高山对峙，崖壁陡峭，而江面最窄处不足百米，江中滩峡相间，水流湍急，形成了独特的自然奇观。长江三峡还是中国古文明的发源地之一，保留着无数古代文化遗迹。古往今来，历代文人曾写下了许多歌咏三峡的优美诗文。

  1994年在湖北省宜昌市夷陵区兴建集防洪、发电、航运、水资源利用等功能为一体的三峡大坝，2006年5月完工。随着储水水位抬高，湍急凶险的三峡江段变得平缓。

- 风光壮美的长江三峡 (图片提供：全景正片)
  Magnificent Scenery of the Three Gorges

Three Gorges of the Yangtze River

The Three Gorges is a section of canyons in the middle reaches of the Yangtze River. It starts from Baidi Castle in the west, which is located in Fengjie County in Chongqing, to the Nanjinguan in the east, which lies in Yichang City in Hubei Province. The Three Gorges is the general name of Qutang Gorge, Wuxia Gorge and Xiling Gorge, with an overall length 193 kilometers. The shape of the Three Gorges is the result of the rising of the crust and the undercutting of the river in this area. The narrowest point of the river surface is less than 100 meters. The high mountains and sheer cliffs erect on both sides of the river and the rocks and turbulent currents in the middle of the river constitute a unique natural wonder. Besides, the Three Gorges is also one of the birthplaces of ancient Chinese cultures and reserves countless ancient cultural relics. From ancient times till now, scholars of different epochs have written many beautiful poems and essays in praise of the Three Gorges.

Construction of the Three Gorge Dam began in 1994 in Yiling District, Yichang City, Hubei Province, and was completed in May 2006. Three Gorge Dam integrates flood control, power generation, navigation and water resource utilization. As the water storage level rises, the turbulent and dangerous section of the river flowing through the Three Gorges becomes gentle.

长江的支流与湖泊

长江的支流众多，从上游到下游主要有雅砻江、岷江、沱江、赤水河、嘉陵江、乌江、湘江、沅江、汉江、赣江、青弋江、黄浦江等。长江流域的主要湖泊有滇池、洪湖、洞庭湖、鄱阳湖、巢湖、太湖等。

雅砻江古称"若水""泸水"，为长江上游金沙江的支流，发源于青海省巴颜喀拉山南麓，东南流入四川省，在四川与云南边界处的攀枝花市注入金沙江。雅砻江

Tributaries and Lakes of the Yangtze River

The Yangtze River possesses a great number of tributaries from the upper reaches to the lower reaches, including Yalong River, Minjiang River, Tuojiang River, Chishui River, Jialing River, Wujiang River, Xiangjiang River, Ruanjiang River, Hanjiang River, Ganjiang River, Qingyi River, Huangpu River and so on. And the major lakes of the Yangtze River basin include Dianchi Lake, Honghu Lake, Dongting Lake, Poyang Lake, Chaohu Lake, Taihu Lake and so on.

干流全长1571千米，落差较大，水流湍急，有"小金沙江"之称。流域内由于地理环境差异，上、中游与下游社会环境差别较大。上、中游地区地广人稀，畜牧业比较发达；下游地区人口稠密，工农业发

The ancient name of the Yalong River is "Ruoshui" or "Lushui", which is the tributary of the Jinsha River. The Yalong River originates from the south foot of the Bayan Har Mountain in Qinghai Province, and then heads southeast into Sichuan Province. After that, it enters the Jinsha River in Panzhihua City in the border area of Sichuan Province and Yunnan Province. The main stream of the Yalong River is 1571 kilometers. With a big vertical drop and rushing current, the Yalong River is also referred to the "small Jinsha River". As the geographic environment diversity within the river basin is distinct, the social environments between the areas of the upper and middle reaches and the areas of the lower reaches are extremely different. In the upper and middle reaches areas, there is a vast territory with sparse population and the animal husbandry is prosperous. The lower reaches areas are densely populated, and the agriculture and

- 岷江边的乐山大佛（图片提供：全景正片）
岷江与青衣江、大渡河共汇于乐山凌云岩下，世界上最宏伟的石刻巨佛乐山大佛就安坐在江边。

Leshan Giant Buddha on the Bank of the Minjiang River
The Minjiang River, Qingyi River and Dadu River combine together at the Leshan Lingyun Mountain, where sits the world's most grandiose caved stone Buddha, the Leshan Giant Buddha.

造福千年的都江堰

　　都江堰位于今四川省都江堰市，地处岷江中游。工程始建于公元前256年，渠首在灌县境内，包括"鱼嘴""金刚堤""飞沙堰"和"宝瓶口"四个主要工程和数以千计的渠道与分堰。鱼嘴是修建在江心的分水堤坝，把汹涌的岷江分隔成外江和内江，外江排洪，内江引水灌溉。飞沙堰起泄洪、排沙和调节水量的作用。宝瓶口因形状有如瓶颈而得名，作用是控制内江的进水流量。内江的水经过宝瓶口流入成都平原，可灌溉农田。整个工程将岷江水一分为二，既解除了岷江水患，又使成都平原获得灌溉与运输之利，成都平原自此成为真正的"天府之国"。2000年，联合国教科文组织将都江堰列入《世界遗产名录》，并评价其"不愧为文明世界的伟大杰作，造福人民的伟大水利工程"。

● **都江堰全景**
Full View of Dujiangyan Weir

Dujiangyan Weir, Benefiting the Later Generations

Located in Dujiangyan City in Sichuan Province in the middle reaches of the Minjiang River, the Dujiangyan Weir was established in 256 B.C. The headwork lies in Guanxian County, and consists of thousands of channels and weirs. The four key projects of it are "Yuzui", "Jingang Dam", "Feisha Weir" and "Baopingkou". The Yuzui (Fish Snout) stands in the middle of the river and is a project to divert the water. It divides the turbulent Minjiang River into an inner channel and an outer channel. The water diverted into the outer channel carries surplus water; the water in the inner channel is used for irrigation. The functions of the Feisha Weir (Flying Sand Spillway) are flood discharging, silts releasing and water volume adjusting. The Baopingkou (Precious Bottleneck's Mouth) gets its name for its narrow shape likes the bottleneck, and the function is leading the water entering into the inner channel. The water of the inner channel passes through the Baopingkou and flows into the Chengdu Plain to irrigate the farmlands. The whole project divides the Minjiang River into two parts, which not only controls the flood, but also benefits the Chengdu Plain with irrigation and transportation advantages. The Chengdu Plain becomes the real "Land of Plenty" thanks to the project. In 2000, the UNESCO (United Nations Educational Scientific and Cultural Organization) listed the Dujiangyan Weir on the World Heritage List, and appraised it as "a great masterpiece of the civilized world and great water conservancy project benefiting the generations".

达，四川省凉山彝族自治州的首府、著名的卫星发射中心所在地西昌市就位于雅砻江边。

岷江发源于四川岷山，全长711千米，是长江上游水量最大的一条支流。岷江贯穿成都平原，自古就是蜀地最重要的河流之一。先秦时期，岷江经常泛滥，给两岸百姓带来灾祸。战国末年秦国太守李冰主持修筑了治理岷江的水利工程都江堰，使岷江之水变害为利，成

- 赣江边的滕王阁
  Pavilion of Prince Teng by Ganjiang River

industry are well-developed. Xichang City, the famous satellite launching center, meanwhile also the capital of the Liangshan Yi Autonomous Prefecture in Sichuan Province, lies right by the bank of the Yalong River.

The Minjiang River originates from the Minshan Mountain in Sichuan Province, the total length is 711 kilometers. It has the most water volume among all the tributaries of the Yangtze River's upper reaches. The Minjiang River flows through the Chengdu Plain and has been one of the most important rivers in Sichuan Province since ancient times. In the pre-Qin period, the floods of the Minjiang River were common and brought miserable life to the people living by the river. In the late Warring States Period, a man called Li Bing, who was the prefecture chief of Qin, built up the water conservancy project of Dujiangyan to control the floods. The project turned the harm of the Minjiang River into a benefit, and the Chengdu Plain also became the famous "Land of Plenty" after that. The Minjiang River bred the rich variety of the ancient cultures on the river sides. The upper reaches belonged to the Qiang people in ancient times, where a great deal of cultural relics of the ancient Qiang

都平原也因此成为著名的"天府之国"。岷江两岸孕育了丰富多样的古代文化。岷江上游是古代羌人活动的中心地区，至今保留着许多古羌人的文化遗迹。

沱江发源于四川盆地西北缘的九顶山南麓，全长629千米，在泸州市注入长江。沱江的源头共有五条支流，并且由于岷江水网交错其间，所以沱江不像其他支流那样泾渭分明，可以说是一条"混血"的江。

嘉陵江也是长江上游的一条支流，发源于秦岭北麓的陕西省凤县，因凤县的嘉陵谷而得名。其向南流经陕西省汉中市，穿大巴山，至四川昭化接纳白龙江，再向南流经四川省南充市，到重庆注入长江。全长1119千米，流域面积近16万平方千米，是长江支流中流域面积最大的一条。

汉江又称"汉水"，发源于陕西汉中，在湖北武汉的汉口汇入长江，全长1532千米，是长江最大的支流。汉江流域降水丰富，水量充沛。上游流经汉中盆地，水流湍急，中游以下进入平原，水流平缓，同长江之间的河港纵横交错，尤其是汛期，常与长江洪峰相遇，

people are reserved till now.

The Tuojiang River originates from the south foot of the Jiuding Mountain in the northwest of Sichuan Basin. The river is 629 kilometers long and joins the Yangtze River in Luzhou City. There are five tributaries at the source of the Tuojiang River. And because of the intersecting with the network of the Minjiang River, the Tuojiang River is not that distinctly separated compared with the other tributaries of the Yangtze River. In a manner of speaking, it's a "half-blooded" river.

The Jialing River is another tributary of the Yangtze River. The river gets its name from the Jialing Valley in Fengxian County. It originates from Fengxian County in Shaanxi Province in the north foot of the Qinling Mountains, and flows south through Hanzhong City in Shaanxi Province and the Daba Mountains. When arriving at Zhaohua in Sichuan Province, it takes in the Bailong River. After that, the river continuously heads south and flows through Nanchong City in Sichuan Province, at last joins into the Yangtze River in Chongqing. The total length of the Jialing River is 1119 kilometers and its drainage area is close to 160 thousand square kilometers. The drainage area of

极易造成洪灾。唐代大诗人李白在诗中描写汉江泛滥："横溃豁中国，崔嵬飞迅湍。"

赣江是长江中游的主要支流之一。其源头有二，西源章水出自大庾岭，东源贡水出自江西武夷山区，二水在江西赣州汇合后称"赣江"。赣江向北流到南昌注入鄱阳湖，后泄入长江，全长744千米，流域面积8.09万平方千米。其中上游多礁石险滩，水流湍急，而下游江面宽阔，适于通航，因此过去赣江沿岸各地是长江下游与两广地区的交通纽带。

黄浦江是长江入海之前的最后一条支流，发源于上海朱家角镇的淀山湖，至吴淞口入长江，全长约114千米。黄浦江流经上海市区，将上海分割成了浦西和浦东两部分。吴淞口是黄浦江与长江的入海口，也是黄浦江、长江和东海三股水流交汇的地方，每到涨潮时，会出现著名的"三夹水"奇观：黄浦江水呈青灰色，长江带来的是夹有泥沙的黄色水流，而东海中的海水则呈绿色，三股水泾渭分明，并不相混，十分奇特。

the Jialing River is the largest among all the tributaries of the Yangtze River.

The Hanjiang River is also called Hanshui, which originates from Hanzhong in Shaanxi Province, and joins the Yangtze River in Wuhan in Hubei Province. The 1532 kilometers long Hanjiang River is the largest tributary of the Yangtze River. The Hanjiang River basin has plentiful precipitation and water volume. Its upper reaches flow through the Hanzhong Basin with turbulent current. The middle reaches and the rest of the river flow on the plain and the current is gentle. In these sections, the Hanjiang River is criss-cross with the Yangtze River. Especially in flood season, encountering the flood peak of the Yangtze River can easily cause flooding. The Tang-dynasty poet Li Bai used to describe the overflow of the Hanjiang River in his poem as "massive flood covers the land with turbulent currents".

The Ganjiang River is one of the important tributaries in the middle reaches of the Yangtze River and has two headstreams. The west headstream is the Zhangshui River originating from the Dayuling Mountain in the border area of Guangdong Province and Jiangxi Province; the east headstream is the Gongshui River originating from the

● 黄浦江畔外滩夜景

外滩位于上海市中心的黄浦江畔，全长约1.5千米，东临黄浦江，西面是由哥特式、罗马式、巴洛克式、中西合璧式等52幢风格迥异的大楼所组成的旧上海时期的金融中心、外贸机构的集中带，被誉为"万国建筑博览群"，现在是观光客的必游之地。

The Bund at Night by Huangpu River

The Bund is located in Shanghai downtown by the Huangpu River. Its total length is 1.5 kilometers. The east of the Bund is the Huangpu River, and in the west side of the Bond there is banking center and foreign trade agencies from the old Shanghai period. The architectural complex is constituted of 52 buildings in different styles, including Gothic, Romanesque, Baroque, Chinese and Western-style and so on, is crowned as the "Building Expo" and a must for tourists.

Wuyi Mountain area in Jiangxi Province. The two rivers combine together in Ganzhou in Jiangxi Province, since then the river is called the Ganjiang River. After that it flows north to Nanchang and inflows into the Poyang Lake, at last enters into the Yangtze River. Its overall length is 744 kilometers, and the drainage area is 80.9 thousand square kilometers. The upper reaches of the Ganjiang River are full of rocks, dangerous shoals and rushing currents. But after flowing into

滇池，古名"滇南泽"，位于云南省昆明市的南部。滇池湖水由海口注入普渡河，再汇入金沙江，故属长江水系。滇池湖体略呈弓形，湖面海拔1886.3米，湖岸线长199.5千米，面积298平方千米，是云贵高原上最大的湖泊。滇池四面环

● 滇池日出
Sunrise of Dianchi Lake

the lower reaches, the river becomes wide enough for ships. As a result, the harbors on the Ganjiang River are important traffic links between Guangdong & Guangxi and the lower reaches areas of the Yangtze River.

The Huangpu River is the last tributary of the Yangtze River before entering into the sea. It originates from the Dianshan Lake in Zhujiajiao Town in Shanghai and joins the Yangtze River in the Wusong Port. Its total length is about 114 kilometers. The Huangpu River flows through Shanghai city area and divides Shanghai into Puxi and Pudong. The Wusong Port is the estuary of the Huangpu River and the Yangtze River, and is where the flows of the Huangpu River, the Yangtze River and the East China Sea intersect. When the rising tide is in, people can see the famous wonder of the Three Clamp Water. The water of the Huangpu River is livid; the Yangtze River brings in yellow stream with silts; and the sea water from the East China Sea appears green. The peculiar thing is, the three streams are totally distinct from each other.

The Dianchi Lake (ancient name "South Pool of Dian") is located in the south of Kunming in Yunnan Province.

- **古滇国青铜贮贝器（西汉）**

  古滇国时期，人们大量使用贝币来进行交易，贮贝器就是用来盛装贝币的器物。一般呈鼓形，盖上雕铸各种人物、动物及其活动场面，造型生动，铸造精致，具有浓郁的地方特色。

  Bronze Cowry Box of Ancient Dian Kingdom (Western Han Dynasty)

  In the ancient Dian Kingdom period, people commonly used cowries for trading. Cowry boxes are utensils used to contain the cowries, which usually shape in drum and are carved with various kinds of people, animals and sceneries of actions on the covers. The vivid appearance and delicate foundry technology fully present the local characteristic.

绕着连绵起伏的群山，湖面碧波万顷，风帆点点，湖光山色，风景宜人，素有"高原明珠"的美称。滇池，是云南开发较早的地区之一，远古时代湖边就居住着称为"滇"的原始部落。战国时期，楚国大将

For the water of the Dianchi Lake flowing into the Pudu River in Haikou and then joining the Jinsha River, it is part of the Yangtze River system. The Dianchi Lake is shaped like a bow. It's the largest lake on the Yunnan-Guizhou Plateau, the elevation is 1886.3 meters, the lake strand line is 199.5 kilometers, and the area is 298 square kilometers. With beautiful mountains surrounding the west side of the Dianchi Lake, bluish waves and sailings dotting the scene, the landscape of the Dianchi Lake is very pleasant, so people call it the "Pearl of Plateau". The development of the Dianchi Lake area was early. In ancient age, a primitive tribe called "Dian" lived by the lake. In the Warring States Period, Zhuang Qiao, the general of the Chu State, led his army into the Dianchi Lake area and established the ancient Dian Kingdom. After the Yunnan Province was established in the Yuan Dynasty, the Yachi Castle by the lake was renamed Kunming, which is now the capital of Yunnan Province.

The Dongting Lake (ancient name Cloud and Dream Pool) lies in the south of the Jingjiang River and is located in the border area of Hunan Province and Hubei Province. In the center of the lake lies

• **洞庭湖边的岳阳楼** (图片提供：全景正片)

洞庭湖畔的岳阳楼为江南三大名楼之一，相传在三国时曾是东吴训练水军的阅兵台，唐代扩建为楼阁。历代众多诗文大家都曾登楼览胜，留下诗赋名篇，其中以北宋范仲淹所作的《岳阳楼记》最为著名。岳阳楼的楼顶陡而翘，层叠相衬，宛如古代士兵的头盔，故名"盔顶"，这在中国现存的古建筑中是独一无二的。

Yueyang Tower by the Dongting Lake

The Yueyang Tower by the Dongting Lake is one of the three most outstanding towers in the regions south of the Yangtze River. According to legend, it was a receiving stand built in the Three Kingdoms Period and expanded in the Tang Dynasty. Many giant poets of all ages used to visit the tower and wrote down well-known poems and prose poems, among which the most famous work was the *Remarks of Yueyang Tower* written by Fan Zhong Yan living in the Northern Song Dynasty. The roof of Yueyang Tower is cliffy and cocked, and has many layers. As the roof is similar with the soldier's helmet in ancient times, it's called the "helmet roof", which is only one of China's existing historic buildings.

庄跻率部进入滇池地区，建立了古滇国。元代建立云南行省后，将池畔的鸭赤城改称昆明，现为云南省会所在地。

　　洞庭湖，古称"云梦泽"，位于长江荆江河段以南，跨湖南、湖

a small and perennially green mountain called the Dongting Mountain, and the Dongting Lake gets its name from that. In ancient times people described it Eight Hundred *Li* (a unit of length, 1 *Li* equals to 500 meters) Dongting. At present, the lake area is 2740 square kilometers,

北两省。湖中心有座小山，常年郁郁葱葱，名叫洞庭山，洞庭湖便因此得名。历史上的洞庭湖素有"八百里洞庭"之称，现在湖区面积2740平方千米，是中国第二大淡

which makes it the second largest freshwater lake in China. The landscape of the Dongting Lake is extraordinary. By the lake, there are many historical and cultural scenic spots, like the Yueyang Tower, the Confucian temple and so on. The literature giant of the Northern Song Dynasty Fan Zhongyan used to describe the Dongting Lake in his masterpiece *Remarks of Yueyang Tower*, "Bordered by distant mountains and fed by the Yangtze River, boundless flow vast and mighty, the weather varies day and night, and the scene changes like Proteus." In Chenglingji located in the border area of the Dongting Lake and Yangtze River, there is a place called Sanjiangkou. Stand in this place and overlook the Dongting Lake, people will witness the spectacular scene of the Xiangjiang River heading north and the Yangtze River rolling to the east.

The Poyang Lake is located in the northern part of Jiangxi Province and is China's largest freshwater lake. The

- 《洞庭东山图》赵孟頫（元）
Dongting East Mountain by Zhao Mengfu (Yuan Dynasty)

水湖。洞庭湖烟波浩渺，风光怡人，湖边有许多历史文化名胜，如岳阳楼、文庙等。北宋文学家范仲淹曾在名作《岳阳楼记》中形容洞庭湖："衔远山，吞长江，浩浩汤汤，横无际涯。朝晖夕阴，气象万千。"在东洞庭湖与长江接界处的城陵矶，有一块叫三江口的地方。从这里远眺洞庭，可以看到湘江滔滔北去，长江滚滚东逝的壮观景象。

鄱阳湖位于江西省北部，是中国第一大淡水湖。全湖南宽北窄，形似一只系在长江腰带上的宝葫芦。鄱阳湖面因季节变化伸缩性很大，春夏之交湖水猛涨，水面扩大，湖区广阔，冬季湖水剧降，水落石出，洲滩裸露，湖面仅剩几条蜿蜒的水道，因此有"洪水一片，枯水一线"之说。在鄱阳湖和长江的汇合处，江水混浊，湖水清澈，互不相融，形成一条明显的清浊分界线，十分奇特。鄱阳湖区降水丰富，气候温润，水草丰美，聚集了许多世界珍稀濒危物种。每年冬季，成千上万只候鸟都会从西伯利亚、蒙古、日本、朝鲜以及中国东

south of the lake is wide and the north is narrow, shaped like a magic gourd tied on the belt of the Yangtze River. The area of Poyang Lake is flexible due to the changing of seasons. In spring and summer, the water level rises and the surface expands; in winter the water level drops sharply and the rocks and sediments appear, only a few channels are left on the surface, which inspired the saying "a vast expanse in high water and a slim line in low water". In the influx area of the Poyang Lake and the Yangtze River a boundary line can be seen clearly, which is because the water of the Yangtze River is turbid and the lake water is limpid, and the different types of water don't mingle with each other. The plentiful rainfall, mild climate and lush water plants gather a number of rare or endangered species of the world. Thousands of migratory birds from Siberia, Mongolia, Japan, Korea, the northeast and northwest of China fly to this place every year to live through the winter, induding the world's endangered bird, the white crane. For this reason, the place is also praised as the "homeland of the white crane".

The Taihu Lake sits on the border area of Jiangsu Province and Zhejiang Province in the south of the Yangtze

● 栖息在鄱阳湖畔的白鹤（图片提供：全景正片）
White Cranes Rest by the Poyang Lake

北、西北等地飞来这里越冬。其中包括世界濒危的鸟类白鹤，因此这里又被誉为"世界白鹤的故乡"。

太湖位于江苏和浙江两省的交界处，长江三角洲的南部。整个太湖水系共有大小湖泊180多个，湖岸线总长405千米，湖区有48岛、72峰，水域面积约为2420平方千米，号称"三万六千顷，周围八百里"，是中国的第三大淡水湖。太湖东邻苏州，西接宜兴，南濒湖

Delta. The whole Taihu Lake system contains over 180 uneven sized lakes, with a 405 kilometers long lake strand line, 48 islands, 72 mountains, and about 2420 square kilometers water area. It's China's third largest freshwater lake and be known as "thirty-six thousand *Qing* (a unit of area, 1 *Qing* equals to 6.6667 hectares), eight hundred *Li* (a unit of length, 1 *Li* equals to 500 meters) circumference". The Taihu Lake is near Suzhou in the east, Yixing in the west, Huzhou in the south and Wuxi in

● 太湖夕照
Sunset of Taihu Lake

州，北临无锡。太湖平原气候温和湿润，水网稠密，土壤肥沃，是中国远古文明的发源地之一，也是古代经济文化的繁盛之地。早在六七千年前，这里就有原始人类聚居。唐宋以来，太湖流域一直是中国最为富庶的地区之一，向来以"鱼米之乡"而闻名。

the north. The mild and moist climate, dense network of rivers and fertile soil determined the Taihu Lake Plain to be one of the birthplaces of the Chinese ancient civilizations and the land of economic and cultural prosperity in ancient times. As far back as six to seven thousand years ago, there had been hominids settling here. Since the Tang and Song dynasties, the Taihu Lake basin has continuously been one of the most wealthy regions in China and is well-known as the "land of honey and milk".

> 长江文明

长江源远流长，早在200多万年前，长江两岸便生活着目前所知的中国境内最早的人类——巫山人。从旧石器时代的云南元谋猿人遗址、安徽和县遗址、贵州观音洞遗址、湖北大冶遗址，到新石器时代的大溪文化、屈家岭文化乃至世界闻名的河姆渡文化、良渚文化，中国人的祖先在这里创造了灿烂的长江文明。

元谋猿人

元谋县位于云南省西北部，濒临金沙江中游河段。1965年，考古工作者在元谋上那蚌村附近发掘出属于同一成年人个体的左右门齿化石两颗，之后还陆续发现了石器、炭屑和有人工痕迹的动物肢骨等。

> The Yangtze River Civilization

The Yangtze River has a long history. More than 2 million years ago, the Wushan Man, known as the earliest human in China, existed by the Yangtze River. From the site of Yuanmou Ape Man in Yunnan Province, site of Hexian County in Anhui Province, Guanyindong site in Guizhou Province and Daye site in Hubei Province belonging to the Old Stone Age, to the Daxi culture, Qujialing culture, the world famous Hemudu culture and Liangzhu culture belonging to the New Stone Age, the Chinese ancestor created brilliant Yangtze River civilization.

Yuanmou Ape Man

The Yuanmou County is located in the northwest of Yunnan Province,

云南元谋的金沙江渡口
Jinsha River Ferry in Yuanmou in Yunnan Province

据鉴定，元谋人生活在距今约170万年前，属于旧石器时代早期的古人类，是中国乃至亚洲最早的原始人类。元谋人会制造工具，进行狩猎及采集活动，而且已经学会了用火。元谋人的发现将中国境内发现最早人类化石的年代向前推了一百多万年。

巴蜀文化与三星堆

巴蜀文化是西南地区古代巴、

near the middle reaches of the Jinsha River. In 1965, the archaeologists dug out two teeth fossils belonging to the same adult near Shangnabang Village in Yuanmou. After that, stone artifacts, calcarenite and animal bones with artifacts were successively found. After appraisal, the Yuanmou Ape Man lived 1.7 million years ago in the early stage of the Old Stone Age. These fossils are the oldest hominid fossils of Asia. The Yuanmou Ape Man not only could make instruments, but also had learned to use fire. The discovery of the Yuanmou Ape Man pushed the date of the earliest human fossils found in China over a million years forward.

Ba-Shu Culture and Sanxingdui Site

The Ba-Shu culture is the material cultural heritage of the Ba and Shu people in southwest China, mainly located within Sichuan Province today. The sphere of

蜀先民留下的物质文化，主要分布在今天四川省境内。其中蜀人活动范围以成都为中心，而巴人的活动范围在四川盆地的东部，以今天的重庆为中心。大约在殷商时期，巴蜀文化进入青铜时代，其文化遗址以四川广汉的三星堆影响最大。三星堆遗址位于四川省广汉市南兴镇，是长江中上游地区的青铜时代遗址，是长江流域早期文明的代表。遗址年代为公元前2800年至公元前800年，相当于中原的夏商

activities of the Shu people was based in Chengdu; and that of the Ba people was in the east of Sichuan Basin and based in today's Chongqing. During about the Shang Dynasty, the Ba-Shu culture entered into the Bronze Age. Among all its historic sites, the most influential one is the Sanxingdui site, which is located in Nanxing Town in Guanghan in Sichuan Province. This Bronze Age site lies in the upper reaches area of the Yangtze River, and is the representative of the early civilizations in the Yangtze

- 三星堆文化青铜凸目面具
Bronze Bulgy Eyes Mask from Sanxingdui Culture

- 三星堆文化青铜头像
Bronze Head Portrait from Sanxingdui Culture

古蜀国的历史与传说

　　长江上游的巴蜀地区，在先秦时期的历史富有传奇色彩。传说最早的蜀王名叫蚕丛，他的部族是古代氐羌人的一支。春秋时期，有位著名的蜀王杜宇，他在位期间大力发展农耕，获得百姓的拥戴。传说他退位之后，隐居于川西的深山之中，死后化为杜鹃。每到春天回暖时，杜鹃就会不停地啼叫，催人播种耕耘。

History and Legend of Ancient Shu Kingdom

The history of the Ba-Shu region in the upper reaches of the Yangtze River in the pre-Qin period is legendary. Legend has it that their first King was called Can Cong, who was from a branch tribal of the ancient Di-Qiang people. In the Spring and Autumn Period, there was a famous Shu King called Du Yu who strived to develop farming and got people's acclaim. After Du Yu gave up the crown, he lived alone in the remote mountains in the west of Sichuan. When he died, according to the legend, he turned into a cuckoo. Every spring the cuckoo crows to supervise people farming.

- 鲜艳的杜鹃花
Bright-colored Azaleas

周时期。在遗址中发现一座城址，其建造年代最迟为商代早期，属于古蜀国文化遗址。古蜀国是与中原商王朝并立的方国，国力十分强大。遗址中两座大型祭祀坑内出土了青铜器、玉石器、象牙、贝、陶器和金器等各类文物近千件。其中金杖、黄金面罩、大型青铜人立像和青铜神树制作精美，形象神秘而夸张，珍贵无比。这些文物为研究古蜀国的历史和古蜀人的生活、礼仪、宗教等提供了极为重要的史料。

河姆渡文化与良渚文化

河姆渡文化和良渚文化都属于分布在长江流域下游地区的新石器文化。

河姆渡文化因首次发现于浙江省余姚县（今余姚市）的河姆渡而得名。经测定，河姆渡文化的年代为公元前5000年至公元前3300年，当时已经形成了母系氏族的村落。在遗址中发现了大量稻谷、谷壳、稻秆、稻叶等遗存，还有一件印有稻穗图案的陶盆，说明河姆渡时期的人们已经开始人工栽培水稻，

River basin. The date of the site is from 2800 B.C. to 800 B.C., which coincides with the Xia, Shang and Zhou dynasties in Central Plains of China. A town site was found in the site, which was built in the early stage of the Shang Dynasty at the latest and belongs to the ancient Shu Kingdom cultural site. The ancient Shu Kingdom existed simultaneously with the Shang Dynasty in Central Plains and its national power was very strong. Nearly a thousand various cultural relics including bronze ware, jades, ivories, cowries, potteries and gold vessels were excavated from two giant sacrificial pits in the site. Among which the gold scepter, gold mask, large bronze statue and bronze tree with elegant workmanship and mysterious and exaggerated figures are the most precious. These cultural relics provide important historical data for us to study the history of the ancient Shu Kingdom and the life, courtesy and religion of their people.

Hemudu and Liangzhu Cultures

The Hemudu and Liangzhu cultures are both New Stone Age cultures spread over the lower reaches areas of the Yangtze River basin.

原始的稻作农业文明已经出现。遗址中发现了大批农业生产工具，最有代表性的是翻耕土地的骨耜，此外还有少量石斧、石刀和舂米木杵等。根据遗址中遗存的大量兽骨和骨制工具判断，河姆渡人已经开始饲养猪、狗和水牛等家畜。在河姆

• 河姆渡遗址出土的夹炭黑陶釜
Black Ceramic Carbon Boiler Excavated from Hemudu Site

• 河姆渡遗址出土的猪纹方钵
Square Pot with Pig Figure Excavated from Hemudu Site

The Hemudu culture gets its name from it being first discovered in Hemudu in Yuyao County (now Yuyao City) in Zhejiang Province. After identification, the decade of the Hemudu culture was from 5000 B.C. to 3300 B.C., when matriarchal villages were already established. Together with a great deal of paddies, chaffs, straws and paddy stems remains, a pottery imprinted with ear of rice was found in the site, proving the Hemudu people artificially cultivated rice and the emergence of the primitive rice agriculture civilization. Large quantities of farming instruments were also excavated from the site. The most representative among them is the bone *Si* (a spade-shaped farming tool used in ancient China) used to turn over the soil. Besides, there are small quantities of stone axes, stone knives and wood pestles. Judging from the large quantities of the animal bones and instruments made in animal bones that remained in the site, the Hemudu people had already begun to feed livestock including pig, dog, buffalo and so on. And the primitive weaving tools excavated from the Hemudu cultural site including the ceramic spinning reel, cloth stick, spindle unit and machine knife suggest that the

• 河姆渡遗址出土的炭化稻谷和稻茎叶
Charred Rice Spikelet and Rice Stem Leaves Excavated from Hemudu Site

渡文化遗址中还出土了陶制纺轮、卷布棍、梭形器和机刀等原始的织布工具，说明当时人们已经会使用原始的机械进行编织。

良渚文化主要分布在太湖地区，因首先发现于浙江省余杭县（今余杭区）的良渚而得名，是长江下游地区最大的新石器文化遗址，其年代为公元前3300—公元前2200年。从良渚文化遗址的各类遗迹、文物可知，良渚人已经从事水稻的栽培，同时还种植花生、芝麻、蚕豆等农作物，而且农业工具的种类和分工也十分多样。

良渚文化墓葬出土的大量随葬品中，各类玉器占90%以上，包含有

people of that time had started to use primitive machines for weaving.

The Liangzhu culture mainly spreading over the Taihu Lake regions gets its name from being first found in Liangzhu in Yuhang County (now Yuhang District) in Zhejiang Province. It's the largest New Stone Age site in the lower reaches regions of the Yangtze River from 3300 B.C. to 2200 B.C. The various culture relics from the Liangzhu cultural site suggest that the people of that time had started to cultivate crops like rice, peanut, sesame and broad beans for example using various kinds of farming instruments.

Among the vast burial accessories excavated from the Liangzhu cultural tombs, different kinds of jade ware

• 良渚文化玉琮

琮是一种内圆外方的筒形玉器，为中国古代重要礼器之一，同时也是权力和财富的象征。

Jade *Cong* from Liangzhu Culture

Cong refers to a kind of barrel-type jade ware shape inside circle and outside square, is one of the important sacrificial vessels in ancient China. Meanwhile it's also the symbol of power and wealth.

• 良渚文化竹节形阔把陶壶

Bamboo-shaped Wide Knob Ceramic Pot from Liangzhu Culture

• 良渚文化墓葬中随葬的玉器

Jade Articles Buried with the Dead in the Tombs of Liangzhu Culture

中国最初的皇冠——三叉形玉器

在良渚文化玉器中，有一种造型独特的器物——三叉形玉器。其基本形制为下端圆弧形，上端是一个对称的方柱体平头三叉，三叉上有的还雕刻着神秘、繁缛的纹饰。到目前为止，这种玉器只在良渚文化分布地区的大型墓葬中出现过，稀有而珍贵，是良渚社会上层权贵专有之物。由于这种玉器通常位于死者头部附近，出土时中叉的上方紧连着一根长玉管，据专家推测，这是一种戴在部落首领头上的王冠。也可以说，良渚文化的三叉形玉器是中国最初的皇冠。

Primary Crowns in China—Trifurcate Jade Articles

Among the jade articles of the Liangzhu culture, the trifurcate jade articles are very special. The basic shape of which is circular arc-like at the bottom end, symmetric cubic flat-topped trident at the upper end, and carved with mysterious and overelaborate designs. So far, this rare and valuable kind of jade article was only found in the large-scale tombs in the Liangzhu culture regions belonging to the upper elite figures of the Liangzhu society. As these articles were commonly placed near the head of the dead and the middle forks of the tridents were connected with a long jade pile when excavated, the experts speculate that they refer to a kind of crown wore on the head of the tribe leaders. In a manner of speaking, the trifurcate jade articles of the Liangzhu culture are the primary crowns of China.

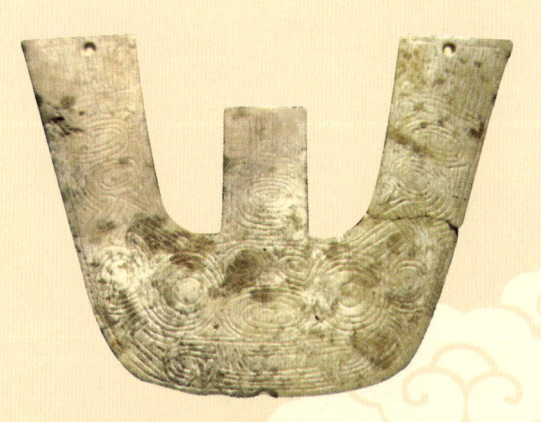

- 良渚文化神像纹三叉形玉器
  Trifurcate Jade Articles with Mysterious Pattern from Liangzhu Culture

玉璧、玉琮、玉钺、玉璜、玉冠形器、三叉形玉器、玉镯、玉管、玉珠、玉坠、柱形玉器、锥形玉器、玉带及环等，种类丰富，而且雕琢相当精美。良渚玉器多为礼器，雕刻手法以阴刻线为主，辅以浅浮雕，并出现了圆雕、半圆雕、镂空等高难度的手法，造型对称均衡，给人一种庄严肃穆的感觉。

楚文化

春秋战国时期，地处长江中游的楚国是长江流域文化最为发达的地方。这一时期的楚文化，不仅以精湛的青铜铸造技术成为长江流域青铜文化的典范，而且在纺

account for over 90%, including jade *Bi*, jade *Cong*, jade *Yue*, jade *Huang*, crown shape ware, trifurcate jade ware, jade bracelet, jade pipe, jade bead, jade pendant, cylinder shape jade ware, cone type jade ware, jade belt, jade ring and so on in rich varieties and with elegant carve processes. Most of the Liangzhu jade articles are sacrificial vessels. Dark engraved lines are the most common carving technique used and supplemented with thin embossment. Besides, some highly difficult techniques including rounded carving, semi-rounded carving and hollowing are also used. The symmetric appearance gives an impression of solemn and respectful.

- 漆木方豆（战国楚）
  Lacquer Wood Square *Dou* (Chu State in the Warring States Period)

• 人物龙凤帛画（战国楚）
Silk Painting of Figure, Loong and Phoenix (Chu State in the Warring States Period)

Culture of Chu

In the Spring and Autumn and Warring States periods, the Chu State located in the middle reaches of the Yangtze River was most developed in the Yangtze River basin. The culture of Chu in this period not only became the paragon in the Yangtze River basin for its exquisite bronze casting technology, but also made outstanding achievements in many aspects including weaving, embroidery, lacquer ware making and wood ware processing.

  Except for daily use, the most famous bronze articles of the Chu State are the sets of chimes, stone-chimes, and *Ding* (cauldron). The set of *Bian*-bells excavated from the Marquis Yi's Tomb in Hubei Province contains 64 pieces. The set of chimes hung on the large bell-cot is complete in structure and grand in scale. It's the earliest super-huge type of musical instrument found in the world with 12 chromatic scales. The vast bronze articles excavated from the Marquis

织、刺绣、漆器生产和木器加工等许多方面都取得了突出的成就。

  楚国的青铜器除了日常器具之外，最著名的就是成套的编钟、编磬和列鼎。在湖北曾侯乙墓出土的成套编钟大小共有64件，分三层悬挂于大型钟架上，结构完整，规模宏大，是现今世界发现最早的具备12个半音音阶的特大型乐器。曾侯乙墓出土的大量青铜器证明了楚国的青铜铸造水平已经十分发达。

楚国的纺织业也十分发达，特别是丝织业和刺绣品尤为突出。考古工作者在楚墓中发现了大批丝织品，包括绢、纱、罗、绮、绦等许多品种，这些丝织品有许多带有刺绣图案，不仅织造精良，而且纹样题材广泛。

楚国生产的漆器包括生活用品、乐器、舟车以及葬具等多个种类，数量众多，性质多样，而且色彩丰富，图案绚丽斑斓，是楚文

Yi's Tomb prove that the bronze casting technology of the Chu State had been well-developed.

The Chu State was also famous for weaving, especially the silk weaving and embroidery. Archaeologists found a great deal of various kinds of silk fabrics in the tombs of Chu, including silk, yarn, net, damask, silk ribbon and so on. Many of these silk fabrics are embroidered with excellent patterns in a wide range of themes.

The lacquer articles produced in the Chu State include living goods, musical instruments, vessels and vehicles, burial equipment and so on. As the lacquer articles are various in kind, numerous in numbers, multiple in characters, plentiful in colors and beautiful in patterns, the lacquer articles can be nominated as the representative handicraft of the Chu culture. The wood ware processing which associated with the lacquer technique was also well-developed. Chu's carpenters made good use of techniques including cutting, chiseling and carving, and

• 屈原像
Portrait of Qu Yuan

化最具代表性的手工业门类。与漆器制造有关的木器加工业也十分发达，楚国的木匠运用削、凿、雕刻等工艺将木器与漆器工艺完美地结合起来。

除了手工业之外，春秋战国时期楚地的思想文化也独具特色，巫文化较为兴盛。这种巫文化背景对当时的哲学和文学产生了巨大影响。如《庄子》一书中体现出的许多瑰丽的幻想都与楚文化有关系。中国历史上第一位伟大的爱国诗人屈原也是楚国人，他的辞赋作品意境开阔、想象丰富、辞藻绚丽、气势雄伟，运用了大量楚地神话传说，带有鲜明的浪漫气息。

perfectly combined the wood ware and lacquer handicrafts.

Except for the handicrafts, the ideology and culture of the Chu State in the Spring and Autumn and Warring States periods were also distinctive, and wizard culture was relatively prosperous, which had a huge impact in philosophy and literature at that time. Many beautiful fantasies in book *Zhuang Zi* were associated with the culture of Chu. The earliest great patriotic poet in Chinese history Qu Yuan was also from the Chu State. His works present wide artistry, beautiful words, wild imaginings and magnificent momentum. He also adopted many myths and legends to bring a romantic atmosphere to the works.

> 长江两岸名城

长江干流所经省级行政区一共有11个，从西至东依次为青海、四川、西藏、云南、重庆、湖北、湖南、江西、安徽、江苏和上海。其中，成都、重庆、长沙、武汉、南昌、南京、杭州、苏州、上海等人口达百万以上的大城市都在长江流域。长江用其特有的自然地理资源，滋养着一座座历史名城。

重庆

重庆简称"渝"，位于长江上游地区、四川盆地的东南部，是中国四个直辖市之一。长江、嘉陵江在这里交汇，使重庆成为长江中上游物资交流的重要港口和经济、金融中心。重庆是一座举世闻名的山城，也是一座历史悠久的名城。两

> Major Cities by the Yangtze River

The main stream of the Yangtze River flows through 11 provincial administrative regions, which are Qinghai, Sichuan, Xizang, Yunnan, Chongqing, Hubei, Hunan, Jiangxi, Anhui, Jiangsu and Shanghai in order from west to east. In these Yangtze River basin provinces, the big cities with populations over one million include Chengdu, Chongqing, Changsha, Wuhan, Nanchang, Nanjing, Hangzhou, Suzhou, Shanghai and so on. The Yangtze River breeds these famous historical cities with its specific natural and geographic resources.

Chongqing

Chongqing (short name Yu), one of China's four municipalities, lies in the

- 重庆朝天门码头

朝天门码头位于重庆东北的嘉陵江、长江交汇处，原是重庆古城门之一，后成为重庆最大的水码头。清代以来，这一带樯帆林立，舟楫穿梭，人群熙熙攘攘，十分热闹。

Chaotianmen Dock in Chongqing

The Chaotianmen Dock is located in northeast of Chongqing at the meeting point of the Jialing River and the Yangtze River. It's the largest dock in Chongqing but used to be one of the ancient city gates. This area has been prosperous and hilarious since the Qing Dynasty.

- 山城重庆的老街十八梯

十八梯位于重庆渝中区校场口，是从上半城（山顶）通到下半城（山脚）的一条老街。这条街道全由石阶铺成，又陡又窄，将山顶的商业区和山下江边的老城区连起来。老街两旁为居民区，带有重庆特有的市井气息和山城韵味。

Old Street Eighteen-ladder in Mountain City Chongqing

The Eighteen-ladder is located in Jiaochangkou in Yuzhong District of Chongqing. It's an old street starting from the upper half city (mountain top) to the lower half city (mountain foot). The street is cliffy and narrow, and completed paved with stone steps, connecting the commercial district on the mountain top and the old city area in the mountain foot at the bank of the river. The residential areas on both sides of the old street provide it with local style and the charm of the mountain city.

upper reaches areas of the Yangtze River in the southeast Sichuan Basin. The Yangtze River and Jialing River meeting in the city determines Chongqing to be the important harbor and the economic and financial center in the middle and upper reaches areas of the Yangtze River. Chongqing is famous as a mountain city and a major city with a long history. Over 20000 years ago in the Old Stone Age, human had settled down in this place. By the New Stone Age, intensive original villages were established by the Yi, Pu and other different ethnic groups. These early inhabitants created the ancient historical civilization of Chongqing.

3700 years ago, the valiant nation Ba lived scattered in the Yangtze River, Jialing River and Hanjiang River basins in the northeast of Sichuan. In the Western Zhou Dynasty, they established their own state and the capital located in today's Chongqing. The Ba people caught fish for a living and were good at dancing. From the Spring and Autumn Period and Warring States Period to the Qin and Han dynasties, their songs and dances were widely popular in the palaces and among the middle and lower reaches

万多年前的旧石器时代，人类就已经在这里繁衍生息了。到新石器时代，重庆地区出现了稠密的原始村落，居住着夷、濮等不同部族。正是这些早期的居民创造了重庆古老的历史文明。

3700年前，在四川东北部和长江、嘉陵江、汉水流域，散居着骁勇善战的巴人。西周时期，巴人正式立国，首府就在今天的重庆。巴人以渔猎为生，而且擅长歌舞，他们的歌曲和舞蹈在春秋战国乃至秦汉时期，都在长江中下游各地及宫廷中受到广泛的欢迎。秦汉时期，中央政府在巴地设郡，农业得到很大的发展，而朝廷在重庆地区的江州城，成为川江地区商业繁荣、人口稠密的大城市。隋唐两宋时期，重庆地区一直较为稳定，经济获得了长足发展。唐代，这里已经出现梯田，农业得到普遍发展。同时，在纺织、井盐、瓷器和冶金等手工业方面也都有进一步的发展。至宋代，巴渝的商品交换兴旺，城镇大量兴起，已成为四川东部的交通要道和商业贸易中心之一。明清时期，随着交通运输业的发展，往来

areas of the Yangtze River. The Qin and Han dynasties set prefectures in the Ba region and well-developed the agriculture in the region. The Jiangzhou City built by the court in the Chongqing region became the major city of commercial booming and dense population in the Chuanjiang River region. During the Sui, Tang, and Song dynasties, the social stability in Chongqing region helped in booming the economy. The agriculture was also developed, like terraced fields exploited in the Tang Dynasty for example. Meanwhile, the handicrafts including weaving, well salt, porcelain and metallurgy also achieved further development. In the Song Dynasty, the exchange of commodities was prosperous and a lot of towns were built in the Ba-Yu region, becoming the vital communication line in east Sichuan and one of the commercial trade centers. Along with the development of the transportation industry during the Ming and Qing dynasties, all kinds of ships busily communicated in Chongqing, and made it the most centralized material distribution center in the upper reaches of the Yangtze River and China's southwest regions.

川江号子

从四川宜宾到湖北宜昌这1000多千米的长江江段俗称"川江",航道弯曲狭窄,明礁暗石林立,急流险滩无数。20世纪以前,江上木船只能靠人力推行或拉纤航行,小船需五六人,大船需二三十人。船工们为统一动作和节奏,同时调剂枯燥艰苦的工作,在拉纤时往往会演唱川江号子,一般由一位"号子头"领唱,众船工帮腔合唱,是一种"一领众和"式的民间歌唱形式。号子头会根据江水势的变化、明滩暗礁的位置、摇橹扳桡的节奏,编创出不同节奏、音调和情绪的号子,时而激越,时而舒缓,具有很高的艺术价值。

Chuanjiang River Work Song

The Chuanjiang River refers to the roughly 1000 kilometers' section of the Yangtze River from Yibin in Sichuan Province to Yichang in Hubei Province. The river is curving and

- 川江边的纤夫 (图片提供:FOTOE)
Boat Trackers by Chuanjing River

narrow and full of endless rocks, torrents and dangerous shoals. Before the 20th century, the wooden boats on the river could only be motivated by manpower towing on the bank. A small boat needed five to six workers, and the large boats required twenty to thirty workers. In order to unify the movement and tempo, and remit the boring hard work, the workers usually sang the Chuanjiang River Work Song. Commonly there is a leading singer and the other workers take charge of the vocal accompaniment and chorus. It's a folk singing form with one man leading the song and the others chiming. The leading singer is able to observe the change of the flow and the locations of the shoals, and accordingly adjust the rhythm, tone and mood of the song, sometimes vehement and sometimes slow. This kind of song is highly valuable in the field of the arts.

于重庆的各类船只十分繁忙，重庆已成为长江上游和西南地区最集中的物资集散地。

清光绪十六年（1890年），重庆开为商埠，各国在重庆纷纷设立领事馆，开辟租界，开设洋行、公司，建立工厂，开采矿山，倾销商品，使重庆及周边地区被纳入了世界市场。抗日战争爆发后，国民政府迁都重庆，使重庆由一个地区性城市一跃而成为中国大后方的政治、军事、经济、文化中心。1997年，重庆成为继北京、天津、上海之后的中国第四个中央直辖市，从此掀开了重庆发展史上崭新的一页。

In the 16th year of Emperor Guangxu's reign (1890) of the Qing Dynasty, Chongqing was opened as a commercial port. Various countries rushed here for selling purposes. Meanwhile, the foreigners set up consulates, concessions, firms, factories and mining constructions, brought Chongqing and its surrounding areas into the world market. After the Chinese People's War of Resistance against Japanese Aggression broke out, the national government moved the capital to Chongqing, and turned it from a regional city to the political, military, economic and cultural center of China's rear area. In 1997, after Beijing, Tianjin and Shanghai,

武汉

武汉市，简称"汉"，是湖北省的省会，位于长江与汉江的交汇处，是华中地区最大的城市。长江及其最长的支流汉江横贯市区，将武汉分为武昌、汉口、汉阳三部分，通称"武汉三镇"。

据考古工作者研究发现，远在6000年以前的新石器时代，武汉就已经有人类聚居。武汉市郊黄陂区发现的盘龙城遗址，是约3500年前的商代方国宫城，是迄今中国发现及保存最完整的商代古城。

春秋战国时，武汉地区属于南方诸侯国之一的楚国，是楚国的军事、经济中心，楚文化的发祥地之一。春秋时期，楚国在楚庄王统治下崛起壮大，成为南方最强大的国家，楚庄王也成为春秋的霸主之一，楚文化的发展达到了鼎盛时期。考古学家在楚国故地发掘出大量的楚文化遗物，包括精美的漆器、青铜器及丝织刺绣工艺品，尤其是青铜器和铁器，其图案之讲究、工艺之精湛令人惊叹。战国末年，强大的楚国被秦国攻灭，楚人留下了"楚虽三户，亡秦必楚"的

Chongqing became China's forth municipality directly under the central government. This is a new historical page of Chongqing.

Wuhan

Wuhan (short name Han) is the capital city of Hubei Province and the biggest city in Central China, located in the meeting area of the Yangtze River and the Hanjiang River. The Yangtze River and its longest tributary Hanjiang River flow through the city area and divide Wuhan into three parts of Wuchang, Hankou and Hanyang, which are generally called the Wuhan Three Towns.

According to the research by the archaeologists, humans had been settled in Wuhan since 6000 years ago in the New Stone Age. The Panlong Castle site discovered in Huangpi District located in the suburb of Wuhan was the palace of an affiliated state in the Shang Dynasty about 3500 years ago, which is also the most intact ancient city of the Shang Dynasty discovered in China till now.

In the Spring and Autumn and Warring States periods, the Wuhan region belonged to the Chu State which was one of the southern vassal states. It was the military and economic center of Chu

- **"郢称"金钣（战国楚）**

  这是战国时期楚国的一种称量货币，黄金制成，正面有压印篆文"郢称"二字，"郢"指楚国国都郢（今湖北江陵），"称"原是重量单位，在这里指货币标度。

  Yingcheng Gold Plate (Chu State in Warring States Period)

  This is one of the moneys by weight of the Chu State in the Warring States Period (475 B.C.-221 B.C.). The plate is made of gold and carved with words of *Yingcheng* in seal character on the surface. The word *Ying* refers to the capital of Chu State (located in today's Jiangling County in Hubei Province) and *Cheng* was a unit of weight in ancient times and refers to the scale of the money.

誓言。秦朝经过短暂的统一，最后还是被楚人后裔项羽所推翻。

东汉末年到三国时期，武汉及其周边地区成为魏、蜀、吴三方的鏖战之地，著名的赤壁之战（208年）就发生在距武汉市164千米的赤壁市江边。赤壁之战后，三国鼎立

and the birthplace of the Chu culture. In the Spring and Autumn Period, the Chu State led by the King Zhuang of Chu rose sharply and became the strongest nation in south China. The King Zhuang of Chu also became one of the warlords of that time. The development of the Chu culture reached its peak. The archaeologists excavated vast relics of the Chu culture from the land of the Chu State including fine lacquers, bronze ware and silks and embroideries. Among which the exquisite designs and craftsmanship of the bronze and iron ware are most impressive. In the late Warring States Period, the powerful Chu State was destroyed by the state of Qin. Before the state perished, Chu's people left the oath "though the state perished, Qin must be destroyed by the offspring of Chu". Dramatically, after the

● 武汉黄鹤楼

黄鹤楼的故址位于武汉蛇山的黄鹄矶头，面对鹦鹉洲，相传始建于三国时期，有"天下江山第一楼"之誉。历代无数文人墨客登楼远眺，吟诗作赋，使黄鹤楼名传四方。唐代大诗人李白曾在诗中写道："故人西辞黄鹤楼，烟花三月下扬州。孤帆远影碧空尽，唯见长江天际流。"

Yellow Crane Tower in Wuhan

The Yellow Crane Tower once located in Huanghu Jitou in the Sheshan Mountain of Wuhan and faces the Parrot Island. According to legend it was firstly built in the Three Kingdoms Period and praised as the "First Tower of China". Countless scholars of all ages used to climb up the tower and wrote down poems and prose poems which spread the name of the Yellow Crane Tower all over the country. The Tang-dynasty poet Li Bai wrote a famous poetry about it:
My intimate bade farewell
To the western Yellow Crane Tower,
Sailing down to Yangzhou in the third month
Amid the misty blooming flowers.
The distant figure of a solitary sail
Gradually vanished on the edge of blue sky.
Only the Yangtze River was seen
Rolling to the far horizon beyond the sky.

short-lived unify, the Qin Dynasty was overthrew by Xiang Yu, who was the descendant of the Chu State.

From the late Eastern Han Dynasty to the Three Kingdoms Period, Wuhan and its surrounding areas became the battlefield in the border area of the three kingdoms Wei, Shu and Wu. The famous Battle of Red Cliffs (208) happened right in Chibi City at the bank of the river 164 kilometers away from Wuhan City. After the Battle of Red Cliffs, the "Three Kingdoms" situation was gradually formed. In 223, the ruler of Wu Kingdom Sun Quan gave an order to establish Xiakou Town near the river located in today's Sheshan Mountain in Wuhan. The town was important in military status and is the first ancient town with a clear record of year numbering within the downtown of Wuhan City.

During the Chenghua Period of the Ming Dynasty, the tributary of the Hanshui River in north of the Guishan Mountain gradually became its main stream joining the Yangtze River. Hankou Town slowly rose within the lakes and marshes area where the Hanshui River connects with the Yangtze River. The three-town structure of Wuchang, Hanyang and Hankou was formed. After

之势逐渐形成。公元223年，东吴统治者孙权命人在今天武汉的蛇山之上近江处筑城，取名夏口城。此城军事地位十分重要，为武汉市区内第一座有明确纪年的古城。

明成化年间，龟山以北的汉水支流逐渐成为汉水入江的主流，汉口镇在汉水与长江相连的湖泽之间逐渐兴起，武昌、汉阳、汉口三镇格局得以形成。明代以后，作为全国性的水陆交通枢纽，汉口镇商业兴盛，来自全国各地的商人云集于

the Ming Dynasty, as the nationwide waterway transportation hub, Hankou Town attracted businessmen all over the country and expanded in scale. During the late Ming and early Qing dynasties, Hankou became the head of China's "Four Famous Towns" and was praised as the "Nine Provinces Thoroughfare".

In 1861, according to the relevant clauses in *The Treaty of Tianjin* and *The Treaty of Beijing* signed between China and the United Kingdon, Hankou was opened to the world,

- 停泊在汉口江面上的外国轮船（20世纪初）
  Foreign Steamships Berthing in Hankou (in the Early 20th Century)

1911年湖北军政府的成立

1911年10月10日，革命党人在武昌发动起义，随即"中华民国军政府鄂军都督府"在武汉建立，标志着辛亥革命的全面爆发。

Foundation of Hubei Military Government in 1911

On October 10, 1911, the members of the revolutionary party crushed the uprising in Wuchang. Soon later the Military Government of the Republic of China Hubei Army Governor Office was built in Wuhan, marking the total outbreak of the Xinhai Revolution.

武汉长江大桥

武汉长江大桥位于湖北省武汉市，大桥横跨在武昌蛇山和汉阳龟山之间，建成于1957年10月，是长江上修建的第一座铁路、公路两用桥梁，曾被称为"万里长江第一桥"。全桥总长1670米，其中正桥1156米，西北岸引桥303米，东南岸引桥211米。从基底至公路桥面高80米，下层为双线铁路桥，宽14.5米，两列火车可以同时对开。上层是公路桥，宽22.5米，其中车行道18米，设4车道，车行道两边的人行道各2.25米。桥身是三联连续桥梁，每联3孔，共8墩9孔。每孔跨度为128米，可以保证巨轮终年航行无阻。正桥的两端建有桥头堡，各高35米，从底层大厅至顶亭，一共7层，有电动升降梯供人上下。附属建筑协调精美，整座大桥异常雄伟。大桥刚建成时，毛泽东主席曾在词作中赞叹道："一桥飞架南北，天堑变通途。"

Wuhan Yangtze River Bridge

It is a double-deck road and rail bridge across the Yangtze River in Wuhan City, Hubei Province. At its completion in October, 1957, the bridge was the easternmost crossing of the Yangtze, and was once referred to as the "First Bridge of the Yangtze River". The bridge extends 1.67 kilometers from Guishan Mountain in Hanyang, on the northern bank of the Yangtze River, to

Sheshan Mountain in Wuchang, on the southern bank of the Yangtze. The bridge is 80 meters high from the base to the surface of the highway. The lower deck is a 14.5 meters wide double-track railway enabling two trains to run from the opposite directions; the upper level of the bridge is a 22.5 meters wide two-way four-lane automobile highway with two 2.25 meters wide sidewalks on both sides. The body of the bridge is made in triple continuous girders. There are three holes on each girder and nine holes and eight piers in total. The span of each hole is 128 meters enabling the large vessels to pass throughout the year. The two 35 meters tall bridge towers were built on both ends. Each tower has 7 storeys including a bottom hall and a top pavilion, and is equipped with elevators. The whole bridge is extremely magnificent and the auxiliary buildings are harmonious and elegant. When the bridge was completed, the chairman Mao Zedong praised in his poetry as, "A bridge crosses over the north and south, turns the natural moat into avenue."

• 武汉长江大桥
Wuhan Yangtze River Bridge

此，城镇规模得到很大发展。明末清初，汉口成为全国"四大名镇"之首，享有"九省通衢"的美誉。

1861年，根据中英《天津条约》和《北京条约》有关条款，汉口对外开埠，英、德、俄、法、日相继在此建立租界。1889年，洋务派官员张之洞推行"新政"，在武汉开办西式的工厂和学堂，编练新军，为武汉的近代化打下了基础。1911年，武昌起义爆发，为辛亥革命打响了第一枪。革命风潮很快席卷全国，最终推翻了清王朝，结束了中国两千年的封建帝制。

南京

南京是江苏省的省会，地处长江下游的宁镇丘陵山区，东连富饶的长江三角洲，西靠皖南丘陵，长江穿境而过，江宽水深，使南京成为天然的河海良港。

南京是一个古老的城市，早在6000年前人类就已在这里耕作生息。春秋末期，越王勾践灭吴国之后，在今天南京城中华门西南角的长干里筑"越城"，为南京建城之始。公元212年，三国时期的吴主

after then the concessions of England, Germany, Russia, France and Japan were established one by one. In 1889, the minister of the Westernization Group Zhang Zhidong carried out the "New Deal". He established western factories and schools, trained the new armed forces, and laid the root for the modernization of Wuhan. In 1911, the Wuchang Uprising broke out, which was the prelude of the Xinhai Revolution. Soon later the revolution agitation spread all over the country, overthrew the Qing Dynasty and finished the 2000 years' feudal monarchy in China.

Nanjing

Nanjing, the capital city of Jiangsu Province, lies in the hilly and mountainous area of Ningzhen in the lower reaches of the Yangtze River. The city connects with the wealthy Yangtze Delta in the east and the South Anhui Hills in the west. The wide and deep Yangtze River flows through the city, determining Nanjing to be a natural harbor.

Nanjing is a city with a long history. 6000 years ago, human had been settled down in this place. In the late Spring and Autumn Period, after the King Goujian

- 石头城遗址

石头城位于南京的清凉山西麓，以山上的峭壁为城基，环山筑造，周长3000米左右，北临长江，南抵秦淮河口，依山傍水，地势十分险峻。城内设有石头仓库，用以储备军粮和兵械。

Stone Town Site

The Stone Town is located in the west foot of the Qingliang Mountain in Nanjing. The town was built surrounding the mountain, and used the cliff as the base of the town. Its perimeter is about 3000 meters. The north of the town is near the Yangtze River and the south is close to the river mouth of the Qinhuai River. Near the mountain and by the river, the topography is very precipitous. Stone storage is equipped inside the city used for reserving army provisions and weapons.

孙权在南京修筑石头城，作为东吴水军的江防要塞和据点。公元229年，孙权称帝后在此建都,定名

destroyed the State of Wu, he built the Yuecheng City in today's southwest corner of Zhonghua Gate in Nanjing, which was the origin of Nanjing. In 212, the King of Wu Kingdom in the Three Kingdoms Period Sun Quan built the Stone Town in Nanjing as the fortress and stronghold of the Wu Kingdom's water army. In 229 after Sun Quan claimed to be emperor, he positioned the capital here with the name of Jianye. It was the official beginning of Nanjing as capital.

In 317, Sima Rui established the Eastern Jin Dynasty based in the former capital of the Wu Kingdom and renamed

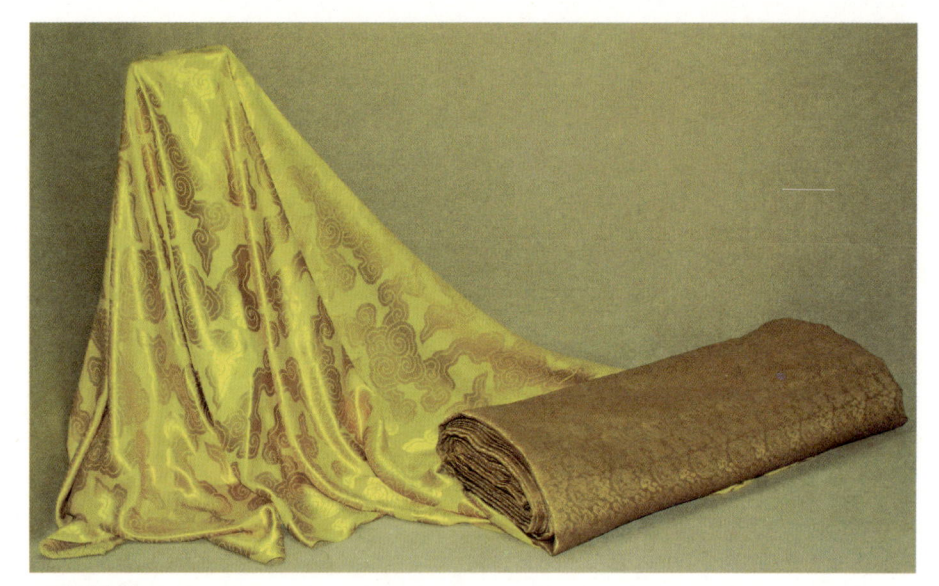

- **南京云锦**

南京云锦与成都的蜀锦、苏州的宋锦、广西的壮锦并称中国"四大名锦",绚丽多姿,美如云霞,被古人称做"寸锦寸金",是用5.6米长、4米高、1.4米宽的"大花楼"木质提花机,由上、下两人配合操作生产出来的。

Nanjing Brocade

The Nanjing Brocade, together with the Shu Brocade of Chengdu, Song Brocade of Suzhou and Zhuang Brocade of Guangxi are praised as China's Four Famous Brocades. The Nanjing Brocade is as beautiful as the rosy clouds, and the ancients described it as "an inch of brocade worth an inch of gold". The brocade was produced by a 5.6 meters long, 4 meters high and 1.4 meters wide Da Hua Lou draw-loom and needed two workers to cooperate the manufacturing.

"建业",这是南京作为都城的正式开始。

公元317年,晋代的琅琊王司马睿以东吴旧都为中心,建立了东晋政权,改名"建康"。此后,南朝的宋、齐、梁、陈四个政权相继在建康定都,南京由此而被称为"六朝古都"。东晋至南朝时,农

it Jiankang. Since then, Song, Qi, Liang and Chen, the four regimes in the Southern dynasties continuously chose Jiankang as capitals. Nanjing is praised as the "ancient capital of six dynasties" for that reason. From the Eastern Jin Dynasty to the Southern dynasties, industries including agriculture, steel-making, paper making, porcelain making and so on

耕、炼钢、造纸和制瓷等农业和手工业都有了重要进步，进而带来商业的繁荣。同时，北方和南方的世家大族，以及佛教和道家的代表人物都会集建康，使其成为当时全国的文化中心。医药学家陶弘景、大书法家王羲之、画家顾恺之、天文学家祖冲之等人，都先后在建康留

had achieved important progress, which boomed the economy. Meanwhile, the influential and privileged families from north to south and the representative personages of the Buddhism and Taoism all gathered in Jiankang and made it the nationwide cultural center of that time. The medical scientist Tao Hongjing, great calligrapher Wang Xizhi, painter Gu Kaizhi and astronomer Zu Chongzhi continuously accomplished immortal masterpieces in Jiankang. Since the Eastern Jin Dynasty, the Buddhism has been popular in China and temples can be seen everywhere in Jiankang City. The poet Du Mu of the late Tang Dynasty described the scene, "The four hundred and eighty temples of the Southern dynasties stood in the misty rain."

In 1368, Zhu Yuanzhang claimed to be the emperor in Jiankang and renamed the city Nanjing. It's the first time of

• **南京栖霞寺舍利塔**
栖霞寺位于南京市东北的栖霞山上，始建于南齐永明七年（489年），是留存至今的南朝古刹之一。

Dagoba in Qixia Temple, Nanjing
The Qixia Temple was firstly built in the Qixia Mountain northeast to Nanjing in 489 in the Southern Qi Dynasty, and is one of the existing ancient temples of the Southern dynasties.

下了不朽的作品。东晋以来，佛教盛行，建康城内外寺宇比比皆是。晚唐诗人杜牧对此做了生动的描述："南朝四百八十寺，多少楼台烟雨中。"

1368年，明太祖朱元璋在建康称帝，改称"南京"，这是南京第一次成为全国的首都。明代初期，

Nanjing to be the nationwide capital. In the early Ming Dynasty, Nanjing achieved rapid development in the economy and culture fields and became the largest city of the nation. The most advanced industry was silk weaving managed by the government and the major products were high class brocade, plain satin, damask silk, silk net, yarn and

- **南京夫子庙**

夫子庙始建于宋代，位于秦淮河北岸，是历代祭祀儒家创始人孔子的地方。以夫子庙建筑为中心的内秦淮河地带，包括秦淮河两岸的街巷、民居、古迹，是南京最繁华的地方。

Confucius Temple in Nanjing

The Confucius Temple was firstly built in the Song Dynasty on the north bank of the Qinhuai River, and was used for sacrificing the founder of Confucianism confucius. The surrounding areas of the Confucius Temple are the most prosperous areas in Nanjing, including the streets, dwellings and historical sites on the banks of the Qinhuai River.

- **南京长江大桥**

南京长江大桥位于南京市西北的长江上，建成于1968年，是长江上第一座由中国自行设计建造的双层式铁路、公路两用桥梁。

Nanjing Yangtze River Bridge

Spanning the Yangtze River at its lower reaches, the Nanjing Yangtze River Bridge was open to traffic in 1968. It's the first double-deck rail-road bridge that was built with solely Chinese design and execution of construction work on the Yangtze River.

南京的经济、文化得到迅速发展，成为全国最大的城市。尤其是官营的丝织业，以织造高级锦缎、素缎和绫、罗、纱、绢为主，尤以织金锦和金银线织成的彩色妆花缎技艺最为精湛。同时，南京的建筑业、

silk. Among which the most exquisite products are the gold weaving brocade and color *Zhuanghua* satin weaved by the gold and silver yarn. Meanwhile, Nanjing was nation-famous for its construction, shipbuilding and woodblock printing industries.

南京与秦淮河

　　秦淮河是流经南京的第一大河，由东向西横贯市区，从西水关流出城后注入长江。城里的东、西水关之间的河段，从三国时期的东吴以来就是繁华的商业区。六朝时，秦淮河畔成为名门望族的聚居之地，商贾云集，文人会聚。隋唐以后，这里虽渐趋衰落，却吸引了无数文人骚客来此凭吊。到了宋代，十里秦淮逐渐复苏为江南文化中心。明清两代，尤其是明代，是十里秦淮的鼎盛时期，金粉楼台，鳞次栉比。画舫凌波，桨声灯影，构成一幅如梦如幻的美景。如今的秦淮河两岸全是古色古香的建筑群，飞檐漏窗，雕梁画栋，加之人文荟萃、市井繁华，集中体现了金陵古都的风貌，被称为"中国第一历史文化名河"。

Nanjing and Qinhuai River

The Qinhuai River is the largest river flowing through Nanjing. It traverses the downtown from east to west and enters into the Yangtze River after flowing out of the city from the West Water

- 夜色中的秦淮河
Qinhuai River Under Moonlight

Pass. The area between the East and West Water Passes has been a prosperous commercial district since the Wu Kingdom in the Three Kingdoms Period. During the Six dynasties the banks of the Qinhuai River became the gathering place of the noble families, great merchants and scholars. Although the place gradually declined after the Sui and Tang dynasties, but countless scholars were attracted here. By the Song Dynasty, the Qinhuai area slowly revived and became the cultural center of the area in south of Yangtze River. During the Ming and Qing dynasties, especially for the Ming Dynasty, the prosperity of the Qinhuai area reached its peak. Beautiful buildings could be seen everywhere. The painted pleasure boats, dainty waves, sounds of paddles and lights constitute the gorgeous scenery. The banks of the Qinhuai River today are full of buildings in antique flavor. The cornices and leaking windows, carved beams and painted rafters, talents and prosperous marketplaces and so on intensively present the style and features of the Jinling Ancient Capital. The Qinhuai River is also referred to as the Historic River of China.

造船业和雕版印刷业也闻名全国。

1853年，太平天国定都于此，改名"天京"。1912年元旦，中华民国成立，孙中山先生在南京就任中华民国临时大总统。1927年，国民政府定南京为首都。

镇江

镇江位于江苏省南部，长江三角洲北翼的中心，因扼守长江、地势重要，得名"镇江"，自古以来就是南北贸易的商埠重地。西周时期，镇江地区是宜侯的封地，所以名"宜"。战国时属楚，称"谷

In 1853, Nanjing was chosen as capital of the Taiping Heavenly Kingdom and was renamed Tianjing. Sun Yat-sen was elected Interim President of the Republic of China, and his inauguration on January 1st, 1912 in Nanjing marked the installment of the interim government of the Republic of China. In 1927, the National Government of the Republic of China made Nanjing the capital.

Zhenjiang

Zhenjiang is located in the east of Jiangsu Province in the center area of the north Yangtze River Delta. Because of the important geographic location

● 镇江金山寺佛塔（图片提供：全景正片）

金山寺位于镇江市区西北，古代这里曾是长江中的一个小岛，清代道光年间始与南岸陆地相连。在民间传说《白蛇传》中，蛇精化成的美女白素贞为了救出被法海和尚困于金山寺中的丈夫许仙，曾大施法力，水漫金山。这也给古老的金沙寺带来一抹浪漫的色彩。

Zhenjiang Golden Mount Temple Pagoda

The Golden Mount Temple is located in the northwest of Zhenjiang City. In ancient times the place was used to be a small island in the Yangtze River and connecting to the south bank in the Qing Dynasty. In the folk legend *The Legend of White Snake*, the beauty Bai Suzhen formed from a snake spirit used magic bringing flood to the Golden Mount Temple for saving her husband Xu Xian who was trapped in the temple by Fahai Monk. The story provides the ancient Golden Mount Temple with romantic mood.

阳"。秦统一中国后，改名为"丹徒"。三国时期，东吴孙权称帝后曾在此地建都，铸造"铁瓮城"，称为"京口"。到了北宋，建镇江府，取"镇守长江"之意。

of guarding the Yangtze River, it gets the name of Zhenjiang (*Zhen* refers to "garrison" in Chinese) and has always been the important commercial port for north-south trading since antiquity. In the Western Zhou Dynasty, the Zhenjiang area was the manor of Marquis Yi, so got the name Yi. In the Warring States Period, it belonged to the Chu State and was named Guyang. After the State of Qin united China, it was renamed Dantu. In the Three Kingdoms Period, the King of the Wu Kingdom Sun Quan chose this place as the capital and named it Jingkou. The Northern Song Dynasty established the Zhenjiang Prefecture, the name of which took the meaning of

镇江三怪
Three Unique Delicacies in Zhenjiang

作为历史悠久的名城，镇江不仅文化发达，而且保留了许多独具特色的传统风味饮食。镇江有民谣说："镇江有三怪，香醋摆不坏，肴肉不当菜，面锅里面煮锅盖。"其中就提到了镇江最有代表性的三种特产。

As a historical city, Zhenjiang is not only developed in culture, but also reserves many traditional delicacies. The folk rhyme of Zhenjiang "the three unique of Zhenjiang, Spiced Vinegar never goes bad, Salted Pork not being a dish, and Pot Noddle boiled in the pot" mentions the three representatives unique of Zhenjiang.

肴肉

肴肉又名"水晶肴蹄"。相传很久以前，镇江城里一对夫妻开了一家小酒店。除夕，妻子上街买回一包做鞭炮用的硝，随手放在锅台上。丈夫腌猪蹄时，误把硝当盐抹在了猪蹄上。几天后夫妻俩发现硝腌的蹄子肉色发红，香味扑鼻。镇江肴肉就此诞生。肴肉皮白肉红，卤冻透明，肥而不腻，香酥鲜嫩。吃的时候再蘸点姜

● **镇江肴肉** (图片提供：全景正片)
Zhenjiang Salted Pork

醋，别有风味。传统的镇江人习惯清早上茶馆泡壶好茶，要一碟肴肉蘸着香醋姜丝吃，所以有"不当菜"之说。

Salted Pork

The Salted Pork is also named "Crystal Salted Pork Trotter". According to the legend, long time ago, a couple in Zhenjiang ran a small restaurant. On New Year's Eve, the wife bough a pack of nitre used for making firecrackers and left it on the cooking bench. The husband mistook the nitre as salt and wiped it on the pork trotter. A few days later the couple found the pork trotter very delicious and red in color. That's how the Zhenjiang Salted Pork was invented. The Salted Pork has white skin and red meat. The meat jerry is transparent and smells like teen spirit. Dotting with ginger and vinegar, the taste is extreme special. The traditional Zhenjiang residents prefer to order a kettle of good tea and a plate of Salted Pork with spiced vinegar and shredded ginger in the morning. So spreads the saying of "Salted Pork not being a dish".

香醋

镇江香醋在中国诸多醋品中别具一格，以优质糯米为原料，采用优良的酸醋菌接种，经过40多道工序，历时70多天酿制而成。其色、香、酸、醇、浓俱全，口感酸而鲜，香而微甜，存放愈久，味道愈醇，而且久放不会变质。这就是"香醋摆不坏"。

Spiced Vinegar

The Spiced Vinegar is very special among the vast varieties of vinegar in China. Choosing the fine sticky rice as raw material, inoculating with excellent vinegar bacteria, going through over 40 processes and lasting for over 70 days, the Spiced Vinegar is finished. The color, smell, sour, alcohol taste and density are excellent. The more time to be reserved, the better the taste, and the vinegar doesn't deteriorate. That just coincides with the saying of "Spiced Vinegar never goes bad".

锅盖面

锅盖面又称"伙面"，在镇江家喻户晓。其做法是将面粉揉好后擀成薄片，用刀细切成面条，下入沸水锅，随即用一只小锅盖盖在面汤上，直至煮熟后捞起，放入调好佐料的碗里即可。锅盖面的特点是软硬恰当，柔韧性好，老少咸宜。

Pot Noodle

The Pot Noodle is also named Gang Noodle, which is widely known in Zhenjiang. The making processes are rolling the farina into slices, cutting the slices into thin noodles and stewing in the burning water, laying a small pot cover on the surface of the soup, taking out the cooked noodles and emptying into the bowl together with condiments. The characters of the Pot Noodle are appropriate mouth feeling and suitable for both young and old.

镇江自古以来人文荟萃。中国历史上第一部文学理论著作《文心雕龙》就是由南朝名士刘勰在这里撰写完成的。唐代著名诗人李白、骆宾王、孟浩然、刘禹锡、杜牧、宋代文学家苏轼、辛弃疾等人都曾在此留下传世之作。镇江民间还流传着"白娘子水漫金山""甘露寺刘备招亲""梁红玉擂鼓战金山"等传说，这些脍炙人口的故事也为古城镇江增添了传奇色彩。

扬州

扬州地处江苏省中部，位于长江与京杭大运河的交汇处，是一座久负盛名的文化之城。

大约7000年前，扬州一带就已经有人在此劳动生息，而且开始了水稻的种植。春秋末年，吴国灭掉了扬州的邗国，筑邗城，并且开掘了连接长江、淮河两大水域的运河"邗沟"。汉代，今天的扬州称为"广陵""江都"，长期是诸侯王的封地。三国时期，曹魏与东吴之间战争不断，广陵成为江淮一带的军事重地。公元589年，隋朝攻灭南方的陈朝，统一全国。隋炀帝即位

"guarding the Yangtze River".

Zhenjiang gathered countless scholars since ancient times. The first literary theory work of China *The System of Literary Criteria* was written by the eminent person from the Southern dynasties Liu Xie in this place. The famous poets in the Tang Dynasty including Li Bai, Luo Binwang, Meng Haoran, Liu Yuxi and Du Mu, and Su Shi, Xin Qiji and so on poets from the Song Dynasty had all written down masterpieces in this place. Legends in everyone's mouth like *The Legend of White Snake*, *Blind Date of Liu Bei in Ganlu Temple*, *Liang Hongyu Beating Drum and Fighting in Golden Mount* and so on have achieved universal praise and increased the legendary of the ancient town Zhenjiang.

Yangzhou

Yangzhou is located in the center area of Jiangsu Province at the meeting-point of the Yangtze River and the Grand Canal of China, is a prestigious cultural city.

About 5000 to 7000 years ago, human had been settling down in this area and breeding rice. In the late Spring and Autumn Period, the Wu State

• 扬州瘦西湖上的五亭桥

五亭桥又名"莲花桥"，位于江苏扬州莲性寺的莲花堤上，初建于清乾隆二十二年（1757年）。

Five-pavilion Bridge on Slender West Lake in Yangzhou

The Five-pavilion Bridge is also called "Lotus Bridge", located in Yangzhou in Jiangsu Province and lies on the Lotus Dyke in the Lotus Temple. It was firstly built in 1757, Qing Dynasty.

后，下令开凿了从余杭（今浙江杭州）到涿郡（今北京）的大运河，连接起黄河、淮河、长江各大水系，扬州成为运河上的水运枢纽，奠定了唐代扬州空前繁荣的基础。

唐代的扬州，农业、商业和手工业相当发达，出现了大量的手工工场和作坊。不仅在江淮之间"富

destroyed the Han State in Yangzhou. After then they built the Hancheng City and the canal "Hangou" to connect the Yangtze River and the Huaihe River systems together. In the Han Dynasty, today's Yangzhou was named Guangling or Jiangdu and was the manor of the Feudatory King's for a long time. In the Three Kingdoms Period, continuous wars between the kingdoms of Wei and Wu made Jiangling the important military city of the Yangtze-Huaihe area. In 589, the Sui Dynasty destroyed the Chen Dynasty in the south and united China. After the Emperor Yang of Sui inherited the throne, he gave orders to dig a great canal from Yuhang (today's Hangzhou in Zhejiang Province) to Zhuojun Prefecture (today's Beijing) connecting the large water systems of the Yellow River, the Huaihe River and the Yangtze River. Yangzhou became the water-front terminal of the canal, laying a solid base for the prosperity of Yangzhou in the Tang Dynasty.

In the Tang Dynasty, the agriculture, business and handicrafts were pretty advanced, vast handicraft factories and workshops appeared. Yangzhou was not only the wealthiest city in the Yangtze-Huaihe area, but also became the largest

甲天下"，而且成为中国东南第一大都会。在以长安（今陕西西安）为中心的水陆交通网中，扬州始终起着枢纽的作用。作为对外交通的重要港口，扬州专设有司舶使，经管对外贸易和友好往来。侨居扬州的客商来自波斯、新罗、日本等各国。日本遣唐使来扬州和高僧鉴真

city in southeast China. In the Chang'an-centric (today's Xian in Shaanxi Province) waterway network, Yangzhou played the part of backbone hub. Being a major external port, Yangzhou was specially set up with the shipping officer managing the foreign trade and friendly communications. Businessmen from Persia, Silla, Japan and so on countries

- 扬州个园

清代扬州的盐商开始营造园林，至今还保留着许多优秀的古典园林，其中历史最悠久、保存最完整的要算坐落在古城北隅的"个园"。个园由两淮盐业商总黄至筠建于清嘉庆二十三年（1818年），园中景色以竹石取胜，园名中的"个"字是取"竹"字半边而来。

Geyuan Garden in Yangzhou

The salt dealers from the Qing Dynasty started to build gardens in Yangzhou and many of the excellent ancient gardens have been reserved till today. Among which the most intact garden with the longest history is the "Geyuan Garden" sitting in the north of the early city. It was built by the Huainan & Huaibei salt industry leader Huang Zhiyun in 1818 in the Qing Dynasty. The garden is famous for the bamboos, and the name "Ge (个)" was half the word "Bamboo (竹)" in Chinese.

- 《衙斋听竹图》郑板桥（清）

扬州八怪是对清代中期活跃在扬州的八个书画家的统称。他们大多出身贫寒，经历坎坷，以卖画为生。在艺术上他们都重视个性化的发挥，力求创新，善于运用水墨写意的绘画技法，以简逸的笔墨来传达物象的精神，画风标新立异、清新狂放。郑板桥是扬州八怪中的代表人物，号称诗、书、画"三绝"。他尤其擅长画竹，这幅《衙斋听竹图》是他的代表作。

Listening to the Sound of Bamboo in the Wind at the Lounge of Government Office by Zheng Banqiao (Qing Dynasty)

The Yangzhou Eight Elites refers to eight artists in the middle Qing Dynasty. Most of them experienced a bumpy life and lived on selling paintings. Artistically they all valued the individuation and innovation, and were good at using leisurely and ordinary painting skills to present the spirits of the objects. Their painting style was maverick and brutal. Zheng Banqiao was the representative person of the Yangzhou Eight Elites and was praised as the master of poetry, handwriting and painting. Bamboo was his favorite, and this *Listening to the Sound of Bamboo in the Wind at the Lounge of Government Office* is his magnum opus.

东渡日本，促进了中日两国的政治、经济、科学和文化之间的交流。

北宋时期，随着农业和手工业的迅速发展和商业的进一步繁荣，扬州再度成为中国东南部的经济、

resided in Yangzhou. The imperial Japanese embassies to China came to Yangzhou and invited the eminent monk Jianzhen back to Japan, promoting the political, economic, scientific and cultural communications between China and Japan.

In the Northern Song Dynasty, along with the rapid development of the agriculture and handicrafts industries and the further prosperity of the economy, Yangzhou once again became the economic and cultural center in southeast China. During the Southern Song Dynasty, the country was stable and the

文化中心。南宋时期，在相对稳定的局面之下，扬州的经济不断恢复发展。两宋时期，著名的文学家欧阳修、苏轼、秦观、姜夔、王令等人都曾在游览扬州后，留下了大量歌咏扬州风光旖旎、市井繁华的诗文名作，使扬州成为人们心目中的"人间天堂"。

元、明两代，扬州经济发展加快，来扬州经商、传教、定居的外国人日渐增多，其中仍以波斯人和阿拉伯人为最。明代时，扬州手工

economy of Yangzhou continuously developed. During the Song Dynasty, the famous literati Ouyang Xiu, Su Shi, Qin Guan, Jiang Kui, Wang Ling and so on visited Yangzhou and wrote down vast masterpieces praising the beautiful sceneries and prosperous marketplaces, making Yangzhou the "Heaven on Earth" in people's minds.

In the Yuan and Ming dynasties, the economy of Yangzhou was well-developed. More and more foreigners came to Yangzhou for business, preaching and immigration purposes.

• 扬派盆景
Yangzhou-style Bonsai

扬州雕版印刷

雕版印刷是运用刀具在木板上雕刻文字或图案,再用墨、纸、绢等材料刷印、装订成册的一种特殊技艺。它肇始于1400年前的中国,开创了人类复印技术的先河,而扬州是中国雕版印刷技艺的发祥地。据研究,扬州的雕版印刷技艺最迟出现在隋代。隋代扬州是全国的政治、经济、文化中心之一,尤其是隋炀帝开凿大运河后,扬州交通更加便利,文化信息传播迅捷,像雕版印刷这样重要的文化信息自然会率先传播到扬州。隋代佛教兴盛,扬州寺观猛增,使扬州佛经需求量增大,推动了雕版印刷的发展。到了清代,扬州雕版印刷空前发展,刻印之书不可胜计,而且刻印质量高、精品多。尤其是乾隆年间由皇帝下令刻印的《全唐诗》,共900卷,代表了当时雕版印刷最高成就,堪称雕版印刷史上划时代的作品。2009年,由扬州广陵古籍刻印社代表中国申报的雕版印刷技艺正式入选《世界人类非物质文化遗产代表作名录》。

Yangzhou Block Printing

Block printing refers to a special handicraft. Firstly carving the characters or images on the wood with cutting tools, and then printing with materials of Chinese ink, paper or silk, at last

- 木刻印版
Wood Marking Board

binding together in book form. It was invented in Yangzhou about 1400 years ago, which started the history of human copying technique. By the research, the block printing technique of Yangzhou appeared in the Sui Dynasty at the latest. In the Sui Dynasty, Yangzhou was one of China's political, economic and cultural centers. Especially after the Emperor Yang of Sui dug the Grand Canal of China, the transportation in Yangzhou became more convenient. Meanwhile, the spreading of information was also enhanced. Important cultural information like the block printing was sure to spread to Yangzhou first. The prosperity of Buddhism at that time boosted the quantity demanded of the Buddhist Scriptures in Yangzhou and promoted the development of the block printing. By the Qing Dynasty, the block printing in Yangzhou reached its peak. Countless high quality books were printed. Especially the *Full Collection of Tang Poems* printed by the direct order of Emperor Qianlong including 900 volumes in total, stands for the highest achievement of the block printing at that time and is rated as a masterpiece in the block printing history. In 2009, Yangzhou Guangling Ancient Books Printing Firm on behalf of the block printing technique was officially accepted by the Masterpieces of the Intangible Heritage of Humanity.

业作坊生产的漆器、玉器、铜器、竹木器具和刺绣品、化妆品都达到了相当高的水平。

清代，康熙、乾隆两位皇帝曾多次巡幸扬州。扬州出现空前的繁华局面，城市人口超过50万，是18世纪末19世纪初世界十大城市之一。这期间更出现了以郑板桥、金农等著名画家为代表的"扬州八怪"及扬州画派。扬州的雕版印刷、民间曲艺、棋艺等均达到了全国最高的水平。

Among which the Persians and Arabians were the most. In the Ming Dynasty, the lacquers, jade ware, bronze ware, bamboo ware, embroideries and cosmetics produced in the handicraft workshops reached a very high level.

In the Qing Dynasty, the emperors Kangxi and Qianlong used to visit Yangzhou many times, and the prosperous of Yangzhou reached its peak. With over half million population, Yangzhou was one of the top ten cities in the world between the end of the 18th century and the beginning of the 19th century. During this period, the

上海

上海简称"申",地处长江三角洲最东部,位于中国东部弧形海岸线的中间,南濒杭州湾,西部与江苏、浙江两省相接,是一座繁华的沿海城市,中国四大直辖市之一。

早在2000多年前,上海地区就已经有人类居住。战国时期,楚国公子春申君在此地建城,称为"申城"。三国时期,上海更名为

Yangzhou Eight Elites including the famous painters Zheng Banqiao and Jin Nong together with the Yangzhou Painting School appeared. The block printing, folk arts and chess art were the highest level over the country.

Shanghai

Shanghai (short name Shen) lies in the easternmost area of the Yangtze River Delta and in the center of China's eastern arc-shaped coastline. Bordering the Bay of Hangzhou in the south, and the two

上海城隍庙

城隍庙位于上海黄浦区,从明清时期以来,一直是上海的经济、文化中心。其中源于清同治年间的老城隍庙市场,集邑庙、园林、建筑、商铺、美食为一体,是上海特有的文化名片。

Shanghai Chenghuang Temple

The Chenghuang Temple is located in Huangpu District of Shanghai and has been the economic and cultural center of Shanghai since the Ming and Qing dynasties. Within the area, the old Chenghuang Temple Market built during the period of Emperor Tongzhi in the Qing Dynasty gathers the city temple, gardens, architectures, stores and cuisines together, is the representative of Shanghai.

● 20世纪初开设在上海外滩的外国银行
Alien Banks Opened on the Bund at the Beginning of the 20th Century

"华亭"。明代，上海地区设立松江府，逐渐成为重要的棉纺织业基地。1842年，鸦片战争结束后，英国强迫清政府签订了《南京条约》，将上海列为五个通商口岸之一。其后，美、法各国相继在上海设租界。此后，上海迅速成为亚洲最繁华的国际化大都市，被称为"十里洋场""东方巴黎"。租界的存在使上海的核心腹地在其后的几十年中始终未被战火波及，加之作为自由贸易港的便利，使得民族产业在上海得以迅猛发展。

provinces of Jiangsu and Zhejiang in the west, it's a prosperous coastal city and one of China's four municipalities directly under the central government.

More than 2000 years ago, humans had settled down in Shanghai area. In the Warring States Period, Lord Chunshen of the Chu State built a city in this place and named it Shen City. In the Three Kingdoms Period, Shanghai was renamed Huating. The Ming Dynasty established the Songjiang Prefecture in Shanghai area, which gradually became the important base of the

20世纪初，中国江南传统文化与开埠后传入上海的欧美文化等融合在一起，逐步形成了既古老又现代，既传统又时尚，区别于中国其他地域文化的自成一体的上海文

- **《蕉荫纳凉图轴》任颐（清）**

  任颐是海派绘画的代表画家，而这幅图所画的正是另一位海派绘画大师吴昌硕的肖像。在构图和人物造型上，任颐吸收了西洋绘画的手法，将人物的内心感受通过笔墨展现出来。

  Enjoying Cool Under Banana Leaves by Ren Yi (Qing Dynasty)

  Ren Yi is the representative painter of the Shanghai School. This painting is the portraiture of another Shanghai School master Wu Changshuo. Ren Yi absorbed the composition and character shaping from the western paintings, better revealed the character's feeling.

cotton textile industry. In 1842 after the Opium War ended, England forced the Qing Government to sign *the Treaty of Nanjing* which determined Shanghai to be one of the treaty ports. After then, countries including the United States and France continuously set up concessions in Shanghai. From then on, Shanghai rapidly became the most prosperous international metropolis in Asia and was praised as the Ten *Li* (a unit of length, 1 *Li* equals to 500 meters) Foreign Markets and Paris of the East. The existence of the concessions kept the core hinterland of Shanghai away from the warfare in subsequent decades. Also because of the convenience of being a free port, the national industries developed rapidly in Shanghai.

At the beginning of the 20th century, China's traditional culture of the area in south Yangtze River began to combine with the European and American culture introduced to Shanghai after its openness, and gradually formed the unique Shanghai culture. Such culture is ancient and traditional, but also modern and fashionable. It's totally different from the other regional cultures of China, and praised as the "Shanghai Style". The words Shanghai Style oriented in the

京剧《打渔杀家》中的梅兰芳（左）与周信芳（右）

周信芳，艺名"麒麟童"，是20世纪上半叶海派京剧的代表人物，他广泛吸取前辈艺人的成功经验，并且大胆对京剧进行改革。与传统京剧相比，海派京剧在艺术上更为写实和生活化，着重塑造人物、表现感情，具有鲜明的地域和时代特色。

Mei Lanfang (Left) and Zhou Xinfang (Right) in Peking Opera *Revolt of the Fishing Folks*

Zhou Xinfang, art name Qilin Tong (Kylin Boy), is the representative person of the Mei School Peking Opera. He widely absorbed the successful experiences from the senior artists' and boldly reformed the Peking Opera. Comparing to the traditional Peking Opera, the Shanghai School Peking Opera is more realistic, and focuses on characterization and feelings revealing, has bright region and times characteristics.

化，又称"海派文化"。"海派"一词始于清朝末年，当时有大批画家为躲避战乱来到上海。来自各地的画家共同切磋，取长补短。同时，由于西洋画开始流行，画家们开始在传统国画的基础上吸纳民间和西洋画的技法，形成了"海上画派"。很快地，"海派"风格从绘画波及戏剧、电影、小说等诸多艺术领域，乃至社会风尚和人们的生活方式。因此，"海派"文化博采众长、锐意进取、

late Qing Dynasty, when many painters came to Shanghai to escape the war and communicate to draw on each other's strength. Meanwhile as the western paintings became popular, these painters started to absorb the western painting skills based on the traditional Chinese painting, and developed the Shanghai School. In no time, the Shanghai Style infiltrated many art fields like drama, movie and fiction, and even influenced the social graces and people's lifestyles. Drawing on others' successful experience and forging ahead with determination,

灵活机动的特点，已经成为上海地区特有的一种文化风格和城市精神。

the Shanghai Style turned from a school of art to a specific cultural style and the spirit of Shanghai.

老上海石库门民居

石库门民居19世纪后期兴起于上海的英、法租界。石库门里弄民居分为新旧两种，老式住宅由江南传统民居按联排式布局而构成，密度较高，最初出现于英租界，由外籍地产商经营，多为乡镇的乡绅所居。其住宅格局沿用传统民居的三合院或四合院布局，宅居前后设有天井。民居前部为主楼，高两层，后部为平房。石库门由门框、门楣和门扇组成，其中门楣处的装饰风格受到外国建筑影响，在细节处理上引入了西方式样。

新式住宅出现在20世纪20年代左右，楼层增至2—3层，层高降低，户内楼梯分户设置，并在平台转角处增设"亭子间"，再往上面就是晒台。屋顶是坡型的，外墙细部有西洋建筑的雕花图案，门上的三角形或圆弧形门头装饰也多为西式图案。住宅的通风、采光条件均有所改善，而装饰更趋于简化和欧化。

• 上海弄堂里的石库门房子
Stone House Dwelling in the Lane of Shanghai

Old Shanghai Dwellings—*Shikumen*

Shikumen originated in the late 19th century within the English and French concessions. It can be divided into two types. The old-style dwellings are constitutive of traditional Jiangnan (area in south of Yangtze River) style folk houses in high density, which were firstly built in the concession of England and managed by the foreign land agents. The residents were most squires from villages and towns. The houses adopted the patterns of triangle or quadrangle dwellings and were equipped with courtyards in the front and back of the houses. The forepart of the dwelling is the main building with two storeys and the rear is the bungalow. The gate is composed of the doorframe, lintel and door leaf. The decorative style of the lintels was influenced by the foreign architectures and presents the western style in the details.

The new-style dwellings appeared in the 1920s. The buildings were heightened to 2-3 storeys and the height of each storey declined. Independent stairs for each household and garrets at the terrace corners were equipped in the dwellings. Above the garrets are the platforms for drying clothes. The roofs of the buildings are sloping; the outer walls are carved with patterns of the western architecture; the western-style triangle or circular arc overdoor are common. The ventilation and lighting of the dwellings are improved, and the decorations tend to be more simplified and Europeanized.

- 石库门门楣上的西洋风格装饰图案
  Western Style Decoration Pattern on the Lintel of the Gate of *Shikumen*

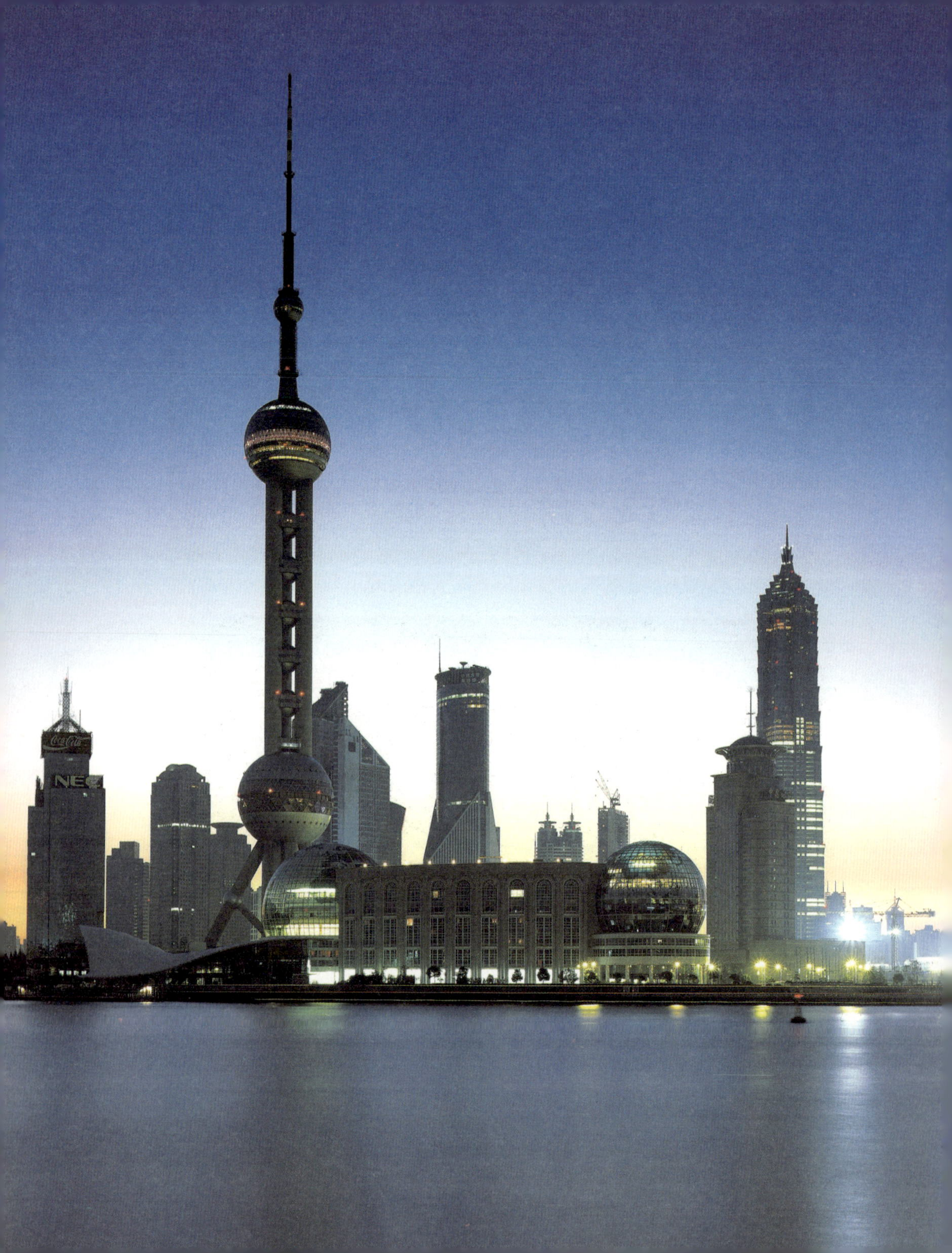
Coca-Cola
NEC

中华民族的母亲河——黄河
The Yellow River—Mother River of Chinese Nation

　　在远古时期，黄河流域就出现了原始先民。他们在这里生活、奋斗和繁衍，创造了丰富多彩的中华文明。历史上，夏、商、周三代，西汉、东汉、隋、唐、北宋等几个强大的统一王朝的核心地区都在黄河中下游一带。这里，不仅有众多的文化名城，还出现了伟大的科学技术、发明创造、文学艺术。黄河哺育了伟大的中华儿女，点亮了千千万万的生命之光。

Since the remote antiquity, primitive ancestors had settled down in the Yellow River basin, they procreated, lived and worked here, and created gorgeous Chinese civilization. In history, the core areas of many powerful unified dynasties including the Xia, Shang, Zhou, Western Han, Eastern Han, Sui, Tang and Northern Song were located in the middle and lower reaches of the Yellow River. Many urban constructions, great sciences and technologies, innovations and creations, and literature arts appeared on this vast land. It can be said that the Yellow River bred the Children of China and lit the flame of life.

> 黄河的源流

黄河，是中国的第二长河，世界第五长河。它发源于青藏高原巴颜喀拉山北麓的约古宗列盆地，经过青海、四川、甘肃、宁夏、内蒙古、陕西、山西、河南、山东等地，最终注入渤海。

黄河源头

早在两千多年前，史籍中就有关于黄河源头的记载。如先秦时期的地理著作《山海经》中就有"河出昆仑"的记载。西汉时期，有人认为黄河发源于于阗（今新疆境内）。隋唐以后，人们逐渐对黄河河源建立了比较正确的认识。唐宋以来，一些人曾亲自涉足黄河源地区，对确定黄河正源进行了有益的探索。历史上人们曾长期将星宿海

> Origin of the Yellow River

The Yellow River, China's second longest river and the fifth longest in the world, origins from the Yueguzonglie Basin at the north foot of the Bayan Har Mountains on the Qinghai-Xizang Plateau, then flows through Qinghai, Sichuan, Gansu, Ningxia, Inner Mongolia, Shaanxi, Shanxi, Henan and Shandong, at last enters into the Bohai Sea.

Headstream of the Yellow River

Early in over 2000 years ago, historical records had mentioned the headstream of the Yellow River. For example, the geographic book *Guideways of Mountains and Seas* of the pre-Qin period said that "the river originates from the Kunlun Mountains". In the Western Han Dynasty, some people suggested the headstream of the Yellow River in Khotan (today's Xinjiang). After the Sui and Tang

● 黄河源头（图片提供：全景正片）
Headstream of the Yellow River

当作黄河源头。进入20世纪后，许多地理学家和专业学者对黄河源头进行了多次科学考察，认定黄河源自青海省境内巴颜喀拉山北麓的约古宗列盆地。这里海拔4500米左右，四面环山，盆地中散布着许多小湖和涌泉，汇聚成三股河流，即

dynasties, people gradually reached a correct understanding of its headstream. During the Tang and Song dynasties, some people visited the riverhead area of the Yellow River and did helpful research on the true headstream. People of that time commonly considered the Ocean of Constellation to be the headstream of the Yellow River. In the 20th century, many geographers and academics conducted repeatedly field trips and defined the Yueguzonglie Basin at the north foot of the Bayan Har Mountains within Qinghai Province to be the headstream of the Yellow River. The basin is about 4500 meters in elevation and embosomed in hills. Many small lakes and springs scatter in the basin and converge into three rivers, the Zhaqu River, the Yueguzonglie River and the Kari River. The 70 kilometers long Zhaqu River in the far north originates from the Chahaxila Mountaion. The river is narrow and the water volume is limited. As a result, for most of the year, the river is drying up. The Yueguzonglie River is the middle one of the three rivers, originating from the southwest of the Yueguzonglie Basin. Its water volume is also small. The headstream of the Kari River in the south is located at the north foot of the

扎曲、约古宗列曲和卡日曲。最北部的扎曲发源于查哈西拉山，河长70千米，河道窄，支流少，水量有限，一年中大部分时间断流干涸。约古宗列曲在三条上源中居中，发源于约古宗列盆地西南隅，水量很小，只是一股股细微的溪流。南部的卡日曲发源于巴颜喀拉山支脉各姿各雅山的北麓，海拔4800米，有5处泉水从谷中涌出，汇成宽约3米、深0.3-0.5米的小河，河流终年有水。这三条河流汇聚为一，形成黄河最初的河流玛曲，注入星宿海。这里大小湖泊密布，阳光之下灿若繁星，星宿海之名由此而来。随后，河流继续向东，流入扎陵湖和鄂陵湖。

黄河分段

从源头到内蒙古托克托县的河口镇的河段，属于黄河的上游，全长3472千米。根据河道特性的不同，黄河上游又可分为河源段、峡谷段和冲积平原段三部分。从青海卡日曲至青海贵德的龙羊峡部分属于河源段，大部分流经海拔三四千米的高原，河流曲折迂回，两岸多

Gezigeya Mountain, which is a branch vein of the Bayan Har Mountains and its elevation is 4800 meters. Five springs gush from the mountain and converge into a small river, 3 meters wide, 0.3 to 0.5 meters deep. The water volume is perennially steady. These three rivers join together to form the Maqu River, which is the primary Yellow River, and flows into the Ocean of Constellation. In this area, a group of lakes scatter densely, and blink under the sunshine like stars. The "Ocean of Constellation" gets its name from that. After then, the river continuously flows east into the Gyaring Lake and the Ngoring Lake.

Sections of the Yellow River

The upper reaches of the Yellow River start from its headstream to Hekou Town in Togtoh County of Inner Mongolia Autonomous Region of China, which is 3472 kilometers long in total. According to the different characters of the river channels, the upper reaches can be divided into three parts, the Headstream Section, the Valley Section and the Alluvial Plain Section. Section from the Kari River in Qinghai Province to the Longyang Gorge refers to the Headstream Section, which mostly flows through

湖泊、沼泽、草滩，水质较清，水流稳定。从龙羊峡到宁夏的青铜峡部分为峡谷段，该河段多为山地丘陵，黄河流经龙羊峡、积石峡、刘

- **陕西延川的黄河乾坤湾** (图片提供：田海峰)
  乾坤湾位于山西永和与陕西延川的交界处，黄河在这里陡然急转，形成320°的大转弯，被称为"天下黄河第一湾"。

  Yellow River Qiankun Bend in Yanchuan in Shaanxi Province
  Qiankun Bend is located in the bordering area of Yonghe in Shanxi Province and Yanchuan in Shaanxi Province. The Yellow River suddenly zigzags in this place forming a big bend in 320 degrees, which is praised as "the first bend of the Yellow River".

the plateau with an elevation of 3000 to 4000 meters. The channel is zigzag with lots of lakes, marshes and grass lands by the banks, the water quality is clean and the stream is steady. The Valley Section is between the Longyang Gorge and the Qingtong Gorge in Ningxia. In this section, 20 gorges are arrayed like the Longyang Gorge, Jishi Gorge, Liujia Gorge, Bapan Gorge, Qingtong Gorge and so on. Steep cliffs live on banks of the river. As the river bed gradually narrowing down, the flow in this section

• 黄河壶口瀑布（图片提供：田海峰）
Yellow River Hukou Waterfall

家峡、八盘峡、青铜峡等20多个峡谷，峡谷两岸悬崖峭壁林立，河床狭窄，水流湍急。洮河、湟水等重要支流在中游汇入黄河，使黄河水

is extremely turbulent and fast. Important tributaries such as the Taohe River and the Huangshui River greatly enrich the water volume of the Yellow River.

The Alluvial Plain Section is from the Qingtong Gorge to Hekou Town, Togtoh County, Inner Mongolia. After passing the Qingtong Gorge, the Yellow River flows northeast along the northwest border of the Erdos Plateau, then turns eastwards to Hekou Town. In this section, the regions along the river are mostly deserts and grasslands, with very few tributaries. The riverbed in this section is flat and the currents are slow. There are large stretches of alluvial plain by the two sides of the river, including the Yinchuan Plain and the Hetao Plain. The Hetao Plain starts from the bank of the Yellow River in the west to Hekou Town in Inner Mongolia in the east, which is 900 kilometers long and 30 to 50 kilometers wide. For the rivers flowing through the plain and the lush water plants, the Hetao Plain has been praised as the Essence of the Yellow River since ancient times.

The sections of the Yellow River between Hekou Town and Taohuayu in Zhengzhou in Henan Province constitute the 1122 kilometers long middle reaches, which are the main source area of the flood and silts of the Yellow River. The tributary systems are extremely rich in this section, over 40 large tributaries flow into the Yellow River. Most of these

量大增。从青铜峡至内蒙古托克托河口镇的河段，属于冲积平原段。黄河出青铜峡后，沿鄂尔多斯高原的西北边界向东北方向流动，然后

向东直抵河口镇。这一段的沿河区域大多为荒漠和草原，基本没有支流注入，干流河床平缓，水流缓慢。两岸有大片的冲积平原，包括银川平原和河套平原。西起宁夏下河沿、东至内蒙古河口镇的河套平原，长900千米，宽30—50千米，由于河流纵横，水草丰美，自古有"黄河百害，唯富一套"的说法。

　　河口镇至河南郑州的桃花峪为黄河中游，是黄河洪水和泥沙的主要来源区，全长为1122千米。这一河段内支流水系特别发达，汇入干流的较大支流有40多条。这些支流绝大部分流经水土流失严重的黄土丘陵沟壑区，每年向黄河输送的泥沙达9亿多吨，把黄河"染"成了黄色。黄河自河口镇急转南下，水流奔腾，将黄土高原切割成两半，左岸为山西省，右岸为陕西省，因此这一段峡谷称为"晋陕峡谷"。峡谷的下段有著名的壶口瀑布。黄河250多米宽的水面在此突然收窄，从17米的高处跌入30—50米宽的石槽里，就像壶中的水通过壶嘴向外倾斜一般，故称为"壶口"。巨大的浪涛在注入谷底后激起一团团水雾

tributaries flow through loess hill areas and deliver nearly one billion tons of silts to the Yellow River per year, "print" the river yellow. The Yellow River zigzags south after passing through Hekou Town, and the rapid streams cut the Loess Plateau into two parts. The left part is Shanxi Province, the right part is Shaanxi Province, and the valley between is called the Jinshan Valley. In the lower section of the valley lies the famous Hukou Waterfall. The name Hukou means bottle mouth in Chinese. The 250 meters wide Yellow River suddenly narrows down in this place, and the water rushes down from 17 meters high to the stone riverbed which is only 30 to 50 meters wide, just like pouring water through a bottle mouth. The scenery of the fall is like a herd of galloping horses, looks quite magnificent and spectacular. The tail end of the Jinshan Valley is called the "Loong Gate", where is 30 kilometers south to Hancheng City in Shaanxi Province. According to the records in the *Journey of Famous Mountains*, "Bold cliffs on the banks like a gate, only loongs can overstep, so called the Loong Gate." In the high water seasons, after the turbulent streams passing through the narrow Loong Gate, the riverbed unexpectedly goes wide

鲤鱼跃龙门

相传每年三月，会有无数的鲤鱼从各条河流游到黄河，汇集到龙门之下，竞相向上跳跃，但每年能跃上龙门的鲤鱼只有72条。鲤鱼一旦登上龙门，就有云雨相随，天上会降下大火烧掉鱼尾，鲤鱼化身为龙。这就是中国民间广为流传的"鲤鱼跃龙门"的传说，而"龙门"一词也由此具有了更多的含义。在古代，人们把学子在科举考试中取得成功比喻为"鱼跃龙门"。

Carps Jumping over the Loong Gate

According to legend, countless carps swim to the Loong Gate and competitively jump in every March of the year, and only 72 carps can jump over the Loong Gate per year. As long as they succeed, flames will fall from the sky and burn up their tails, incarnating the carps into loongs. The folk story Carps Jumping over the Loong Gate endows more implications of the words Loong Gate. In ancient times, people described the students succeeding in the imperial competitive examinations as Carps Jumping over the Loong Gate.

- 古建筑墙壁上的"鲤鱼跃龙门"砖雕
  Tile Carving of Carps Jumping over the Loong Gate on the Ancient Architecture Wall

烟云，声如雷鸣，景色奇丽壮观。晋陕峡谷的末端称为"龙门"，位于陕西韩城市北约30千米处，据《名山记》记载这里："两岸皆断山绝壁，相对如门，唯神龙可越，故曰龙门。"每逢黄河水量大时，龙门水流湍急，汹涌澎湃，穿越这个狭长的通道。涌出龙门后，河床陡然变宽，水势也变得平缓，前后反差巨大。唐代大诗人李白曾在诗中写道："黄河西来决昆仑，咆哮万里触龙门。"

黄河干流自桃花峪以下为黄河下游，长786千米，河道宽浅，支流很少，水势平缓，所以泥沙淤积非常严重，河床不断抬高。河道滩面一般高出地面3—5米，有些河段甚至高出10米，水流全靠两岸堤防控制，成为世界著名的"地上悬河"。

黄河下游冲积平原是中国第二大平原——华北平原的重要组成部分，面积达25万平方千米。平原地势大体以黄河大堤为分水岭。大堤以北为黄河平原，属海河流域；大堤以南为黄淮平原，属淮河流域。黄河的入海口位于山东省东营市黄

and the flow of water slows down. The famous poet of the Tang Dynasty Li Bai described the scenery in his poem, "The Yellow River rushed down the Kunlun Mountains from the west, roaring ten thousand miles to the Loong Gate."

The section from Taohuayu to the river mouth is the lower reaches of the Yellow River, which is 786 kilometers long. With few tributaries in this section, the riverbed is wide and shallow, and the water flow is slow. As a result, more and more sediments accumulate, resulting in the rise of the riverbed. The surface of the river is commonly 3 to 5 meters higher than the land, and in some sections the fall even exceeds 10 meters. People built levees to prevent the Yellow River from breaching. The Yellow River becomes the world-famous "river above ground".

The alluvial plain in the lower reaches of the Yellow River is the important constituent part of China's second largest plain the North China Plain. The area of the alluvial plain is 250 thousand square kilometers and the topography can be generally divided into two parts by the Yellow River Dyke. The north of the dyke is the Yellow River Plain belonging to the Haihe River basin. The south of the dyke is the Huanghuai

● 黄河入海口的湿地景观（图片提供：FOTOE）
Wetland Landscape of Yellow River Estuary

河口镇，地处渤海湾和莱州湾的交汇处，由于每年要承受10亿吨的泥沙，黄河三角洲的淤积延伸速度很快，面积还在不断地扩大。

Plain, which belongs to the Huaihe River basin. The river mouth of the Yellow river is located in Huanghekou Town in Dongying City in Shandong Province, at the bordering area of the Bohai Bay and the Laizhou Bay. With one billion tons of silts carrying to the Yellow River Delta per year, the area of which is continuously expanding.

善变的黄河

由于黄土高原水土流失严重，黄河是世界上含沙量最大的河流。下游泥沙淤积，河床抬升，逐渐变成地上悬河，造成了黄河"善决善徙"的特点。东汉以前，黄河中下游的河道大致沿太行山东麓斜向东北，于今天津附近入海。公元前602年，黄河决宿胥口（今河南淇县东南），这是有记载以来黄河的第一次大改道。秦汉时期，人们开始在黄河下游筑造堤防。公元11年，黄河于魏郡（今河北省南部）决口，形成第二次大改道。直至东汉永平十二年（69年），官员王景主持修堤，才重新固定了黄河中下游河道。此后数百年间，黄河河道基本稳定。但隋唐以后，决口

- 《黄河图》（清）【局部】
  该图细致地描绘了黄河从中游的黄河、渭河交汇口到入海口这一河段的形势，以及流经沿岸城市的位置。

Picture of Yellow River [Part] (Qing Dynasty)
The painting portrays the Yellow River from its meeting point with the Weihe River in the middle reaches to its river mouth in detail, and summarizes the relative cities positions by the river.

泛滥的记载又逐渐增多。北宋庆历八年（1048年），黄河在今河南濮阳附近决口，河道北移至今天津以东入海。南宋建炎二年（1128年），宋军为阻挡金兵南侵，掘开黄河岸堤，河水南流，从淮河河口入海。明弘治五年（1492年）至八年（1495年），黄河连续决口，形成第五次大改道。明代后期，著名水利专家潘季驯主张固定河道，"以堤束水，以水攻沙"。他的治河方略在明末清初得到贯彻，维持了黄河河道的基本稳定。清代中期以后，朝廷政局腐败，河防日渐废弛。清咸丰五年（1855年），黄河再次于今河南兰考附近决口，河水北至山东由大清河入海，这是黄河历史上的第六次大改道。从那时到现在，黄河下游的河道基本固定下来。

Capricious Yellow River

For the serious soil erosion of the Loess Plateau, the Yellow River is the most sediment-laden river in the world. The sediments accumulating in the lower reaches result in the riverbed rising. The Yellow River becomes the "river above ground", and has the characters of "easy breaching and easy moving". Before the Eastern Han Dynasty, the channel in the middle and lower reaches of the Yellow River roughly flowed northeast along with the east foot of the Taihang Mountains and entered into the sea near today's Tianjin. In 602 B.C., the Yellow River breached in Suxukou (southeast of today's Qixian County in Henan Province), which was the first large diversion of the Yellow River in record. During the Qin and Han dynasties, people started to build the dykes by the lower reaches of the Yellow River. In 11 A.D., the Yellow River breached again in Weijun Prefecture (south of today's Hebei Province) and formed the second large diversion. Till 69 A.D. in Eastern Han Dynasty the officer Wang Jing managed to build the dyke and resettled the channel of the Yellow River in its middle and lower reaches. After then in centuries' time the channel was basically stable. But after the Sui and Tang dynasties, records of breaching gradually increased. In 1048 in the Northern Song Dynasty, the Yellow River breached near today's Puyang in Henan Province, and the river mouth rechanneled north to the east of today's Tianjin. In 1128 in the Southern Song Dynasty, the Song army destroyed the dyke to stop the invasion of the Jin-dynasty army. As a result, the river flowed south and entered into the sea by the river mouth of the Huaihe River. From 1492 to 1495 in the Ming Dynasty, the Yellow River breached several times and formed the fifth large diversion. In the late Ming Dynasty, the famous water conservancy expert Pan Jixun suggested to fix the channel by "restraining the water with dyke and treating the silts with water". His project was implemented during the late Ming and early Qing dynasties, and basically steadied the channel of the Yellow River. After the middle Qing Dynasty, the imperial court was corrupt and the dyke was lax. Once again, in 1855 in the Qing Dynasty, the Yellow River breached near today's Lankao in Henan Province. The river flowed to Shandong and entered into the sea by the river mouth of the Daqing River, forming the sixth large diversion of the Yellow River in history. Since then, the lower reaches channel of the Yellow River has been generally stable.

黄河的支流与湖泊

黄河主要的支流有白河、黑河、湟水、祖厉河、清水河、大黑河、窟野河、无定河、汾河、渭河、洛河、沁河、大汶河等。黄河流域的天然湖泊较少，主要有扎陵湖、鄂陵湖、乌梁素海、东平湖等。

洮河是黄河上游右岸的一条重要支流，发源于青海的西倾山，洮河发源后大体顺着西秦岭自西向东流，到达岷县后，急转西北再向北流，于永靖县注入刘家峡水库，因而干流呈"L"形，全长673千米。洮河流域地处青藏高原东北边缘和黄土高原西部，兼有这两大地区的特点。其上游为河源草原区，中游为土石山林区和黄土丘陵区，大多数地区都是草场辽阔、森林茂密的地方，水源涵养条件好。下游属黄土丘陵区，沟壑纵横，植被稀少，黄土裸露，水土流失严重。一到冬天，洮河上就会出现"洮水流珠"的奇观。这是由于洮河上游山岩险峻，在寒冷的深冬，溅起的水珠会立刻冻结为冰珠落入水中，浮在河面上随着河水奔腾流淌。河面上一

Tributaries and Lakes of the Yellow River

The main tributaries of the Yellow River include Baihe River, Heihe River, Huangshui River, Zuli River, Qingshui River, Dahei River, Kuye River, Wuding River, Fenhe River, Weihe River, Luohe River, Qinhe River, Dawen River and so on. The natural lakes in the Yellow River basin are few, mainly including Gyaring Lake, Ngoring Lake, Ulansuhai Lake, Dongping Lake and so on.

The Taohe River is an important tributary in the upper reaches of the Yellow River on its right bank, orienting from the Xiqing Mountain in Qinghai Province, and generally flowing from west to east along with the West Qinling Mountains. After reaching Minxian County, the river zigzags northwest and enters the Liujiaxia Reservoir in the north. The main stream is in "L" shape and 673 kilometers long. The Taohe basin stretches from the northeast edge of the Qinghai-Xizang Plateau to the west of the Loess Plateau, combining the characters of the both plateaus. Its upper reaches areas are the riverhead prairies and the middle reaches areas are composed of the Tushishan Forests and the loess hills areas. Most regions of these two sections had vast meadows and thick forests, where

- 洮河石砚

   砚台是中国古人用来研墨的一种文具，以石质为多。洮河砚用于甘肃卓尼县的洮河河底的洮河石制成，由于长年被水浸蚀，石质细腻，色泽碧绿，石面呈现微黑色的水波状花纹，是中国四大名砚之一。

Taohe Inkstone

Inkstone is a variety of writing material used for rolling ink in ancient China, and mostly made in stone. The Taohe Inkstones were made in Taohe stones produced in the river bottom of the Taohe River in Zhuoni County in Gansu Province. After long time's eroding by the water, the quality of the stones is exquisite and dark green in color. Dusk water wave shape patterns can be seen on the surface of the stones. The Taohe Inkstone is praised as one of the Four Top Inkstones of China.

簇簇的珍珠一般的冰珠滚圆晶亮、玲珑剔透，在阳光下显得璀璨夺目，颇为美丽壮观。

湟水是黄河上游左岸的一条大支流，发源于青海海晏县的包呼图山南麓，流经西宁，于甘肃西固达川汇入黄河，全长374千米。湟水位于黄河流域西北隅，处于青藏高原与黄土高原的交接地带，地质条件复杂，因而水系构造十分独特。流域地貌的主要格局是由北西走向的三条相互平行山脉及其所夹的两条谷地组成。湟水谷地是青藏高原、西北干旱区与黄土高原三大地域单元的接合部，海拔较低，气候温和，土地肥沃，是青海省开发较早

the water conservation condition is well. The lower reaches areas of the Taohe River basin are the loess hills areas, where criss-cross ravines and gullies exist, the vegetation is rare and the soil is exposed. The soil erosion in this region is serious. In winter, wonders of the Pearls Floating in Taohe River can be seen, which is because the droplets from the high cliffs in cold winter immediately freeze before falling into the water and floating on the roaring river. The clusters of ice crystals shine on the river like the pearls under the sunlight. The scenery is beautiful and spectacular.

　　The Huangshui River is an important tributary in the upper reaches of the Yellow River on its left bank, which orients from the south side of the Baohutu Mountain in Haiyan County in Qinghai Province. The river flows through Xining and enters into the Yellow River in Dachuan Town, Xigu District of

的地区。青海省的省会西宁就位于湟水中游的河谷盆地，是青藏高原的东方门户，地理位置十分重要，自古有"西海锁钥"之称。西宁古称"湟中"，具有2000多年的历史，曾是西汉将军赵充国屯田的基地，也是丝绸之路上的重要城镇。汉、藏、蒙古、土、回等多个民族在此聚居，各民族文化在此并存发

Lanzhou City in Gansu Province. The total length of the river is 374 kilometers. The Huangshui River is located in the northwest of the Yellow River basin, at the bordering area of the Qinghai-Xizang Plateau and the Loess Plateau. For the unique structure of the water system, the geological conditions of the river basin are complex. The main structure of the landform within the basin is

• **湟水流经西宁市区**（图片提供：FOTOE）
Huangshui River Flowing Through the Xi'ning Downtown

塔尔寺

　　塔尔寺位于青海湟中莲花山的山坳中，是藏传佛教格鲁派的六大寺院之一。塔尔寺初建时只有一座纯银镀金的圣塔，后几经扩建，目前共有大小建筑1000多座，殿宇僧舍4500多间，规模宏大。塔尔寺内收藏有大量极其珍贵的佛教文物，其中壁画、堆绣、酥油花被誉为"塔尔寺三绝"。

- **青海湟中塔尔寺八白塔** (图片提供：全景正片)

八白塔建于1776年，每座塔的底边周长为9.4米，高6.4米，塔身是由白灰抹面，底座由青砖砌成，腰部装饰有经文和佛龛。

Eight White Towers of Ta'er Temple in Huangzhong, Qinghai Province

The Eight White Towers were built to praise the eight merits of Shakyamuni Buddha in 1776. The bottom of each tower is 9.4 meters long and 6.4 meters high. The tower bodies are wiped with lime, the bottoms are built by black bricks, and the waists are decorated with scriptures and shrines.

Ta'er Temple

The Ta'er Temple is located in the ravine of the Lotus Mountain in Huangzhong in Qinghai Province, is one of the six major temples of the Geluk Sect of the Zang Buddhism. When first built, the temple was only a silver gold-plating saint tower. After several extensions till now, there have been over 1000 buildings and over 4500 rooms, the scale is grand. The Ta'er Temple reserves vast extremely precious Buddhist relics, among which the murals, barbola and butter sculptures are praised as the Three Treasures of Ta'er Temple.

展，具有地方特色的民俗、服饰、文化艺术绚丽多姿。

无定河是黄河中游右岸的一条支流，发源于陕西北部的白于山北麓，流经内蒙古鄂尔多斯市乌审旗，流向东北，后转向东流，于陕西清涧县河口村注入黄河，全长491千米。无定河流域地处黄土高原北部和毛乌素沙漠边缘，水土流失严重，河水含沙量大，平均每年输入黄河的泥沙达2.23亿吨。秦汉时期，无定河流域还是一片森林茂密、水草丰盛的宝地，农牧生产都十分发达。"无定河"这个名称最早于唐代中叶出现在历史文献中。这是由于河水中带有大量泥沙，逐渐沉淀于河床，使河流经常决口改道，难

composed of three paralleled northwest-trending mountains and the two valleys between them. The Huangshui Valley is the combination of the Qinghai-Xizang Plateau region, the arid region of Northwest China and the Loess Plateau region. With low elevation, mild climate and fertile land, it's an early developed area in Qinghai Province. The capital of Qinghai Province Xi'ning, meanwhile the eastern portal of the Qinghai-Xizang Plateau, is located right in the middle reaches basin of the Huangshui River. The geographical position of Xi'ning is very important, which has been praised as the "key of the west" since ancient times. Xi'ning was named Huangzhong in the past and has over 2000 years of history. It used to be the military cultivation base

以稳定，故称"无定"。两岸的地形地貌逐渐形成了风沙滩地、丘陵沟壑，呈现出一派荒凉景象。唐朝诗人陈陶的《陇西行》写道："誓扫匈奴不顾身，五千貂锦丧胡尘。可怜无定河边骨，犹是春闺梦里人。"

汾河发源于山西省神池县太平庄乡西岭村，纵贯山西省境中部，流经太原和临汾两大盆地，于万荣县汇入黄河，干流长713千米，是黄河第二大支流，也是山西省的最大河流。汾河两岸在河水的冲击下形成了许多谷地，山西许多重要工业城市，如太原、榆次、临汾、侯马等，均集中分布在汾河流域的两大谷地中。据史料记载，汾河水流量曾经非常大，公元前647年，春秋时期的晋国发生饥荒，晋惠公向一河之隔的秦国求援，秦穆公发动"泛舟之役"，派运粮的船队经汾河直抵晋国都城。西汉时，汉武帝曾乘坐楼船从汾河逆流而上，写下了"泛楼船兮济汾河，横中流兮扬素波"的诗句。从隋唐到宋辽时期，山西的粮食和山上的奇松古木经汾河流入黄河、渭河，再经漕

of the general Zhao Chongguo in the Western Han Dynasty, and also a major city on the Silk Road. Many ethnic groups including Han, Zang, Mongolian, Tu, Hui and so on settle here. Different ethnic groups coexist and develop together with the gorgeous and colorful local folk customs, costumes and cultural arts.

The Wuding River is a tributary in the middle reaches of the Yellow River on its right bank orienting from the north foot of the Baiyu Mountain in north Shaanxi Province. The river flows through Wushen Banner of Erdos City in Innor Mongolia and turns northeast, after then turns east and enters into the Yellow River in Hekou village in Jingjian County in Shaanxi Province. The overall length of the river is 491 kilometers. The Wuding River basin is located in the north Loess Plateau and the edge of Maowusu Desert where the soil erosion is serious. The river is rich in silts and imports 223 million tons of silts into the Yellow River of average per year. During the Qin and Han dynasties, the Wuding River basin was still a field of fortune with thick forests and abundant water plants, when the husbandry was well-developed. The name of Wuding (means instability in Chinese) first emerged

无定河与黄河的汇流处（图片提供：全景正片）
Meeting Point of the Wuding River and the Yellow River

in the historical records in the middle Tang Dynasty, for the vast silts in the river gradually settling on the riverbed and causing frequent breaches and rechanneling. As the sand beaches and hill-gullies extended, the geomorphology gradually became desolate. The poet of the Tang Dynasty Chen Tao used to describe in his work *Touring in West Gansu,* "Five thousand soldiers selflessly sacrifice for the sweeping of Huns, the pathetic bones by the Wuding River dream for their lovers."

The Fenhe River originates from Xiling Village, Taipingzhuang Township, Shenchi County, Shanxi Province. The river flows through the central area of Shanxi Province and the two basins of Taiyuan and Linfen, and enters into the Yellow River in Wanrong County. It's the second longest tributary of the Yellow River and the largest river in Shanxi Province, the main stream of it is 713 kilometers long. On the banks of the Fenhe River exist lots of valleys formed by the impact of the water. Many major industrial cities including Taiyuan, Yuci, Linfen, Houma and so on are scattered in the two major valleys of the Fenhe River basin. According to the historical records, the water volume of the Fenhe River

• 汾河边平遥古城的古市楼

平遥地处汾河东岸、太原盆地的西南端，是一座具有2700多年历史的古城，迄今还较为完好地保留着明清时期的基本风貌。

Ancient Market Tower in Pingyao Old City by the Fenhe River

Pingyao is located in the east side of the Fenhe River and southwest of the Taiyuan Basin, and is an ancient city with over 2700 years history. The townscape of the Ming and Qing dynasties was well reserved till now.

used to be rich. In 647 B.C., the Jin State in the Spring and Autumn Period was suffering from famine. The King Hui of Jin asked for help from the State of Qin on the other side of the river. The King Mu of Qin dispatched victualer directly to the capital of Jin State through the Fenhe River. In the Western Han Dynasty, the Emperor Wu of Han used to travel by ship against the current of the Fenhe River and wrote the poem of "sailing ship in the Fenhe River, overflowing the waves against the currents". From the Sui and Tang dynasties to the Song and Liao dynasties, the grains in Shanxi and old pines from the mountains were shipped through the Fenhe River to the Yellow River and Weihe River, and finally arrived at Chang'an, mentioned in the historical records as the "thousand pines down the Fenhe River". However, for the geological accidents and effects of human activities, and as the population continuously increased since the Ming and Qing dynasties, the water volume of the Fenhe River has largely declined.

The Weihe River is located in the bottom end of the Yellow River hinterland, and is the largest tributary and carries the most quantity of silts into the Yellow River. 87 cities and towns in

黄河边的窑洞

　　黄河中上游的很大一部分干流和支流都流经黄土高原。黄土高原上的黄土层非常厚，而且具有壁立不倒的特性。当地人利用高原有利的地形，凿洞而居，创造了窑洞建筑。窑洞属于穴居形式，内部采用的是拱顶式的构筑，把顶部压力一分为二，分至两侧，重心稳定，使窑洞有着极强的稳固性。当地民间流传着"有百年不漏的窑洞，没有百年不漏的房厦"的民谚。

　　窑洞一般是在山崖和土坡的坡面上向内挖掘，形成靠崖式窑洞。有一些富裕人家将窑洞与一般住宅相结合，后部是窑洞，前部留出空地建造平房，再用院落围合，形成窑洞式的四合院。还有在平地向下挖掘成为一个方形大坑，再在四面坑壁上向内挖掘出窑洞的下沉式窑洞，这也可以看作是一种四面房屋的四合院。

• 黄土高原上的窑洞民居
（图片提供：田海峰）
Cave Dwelling Residents on the Loess Plateau

Cave Dwellings by the Yellow River

Most of the main streams and tributaries in the upper and middle reaches of the Yellow River flow through the Loess Plateau. The loess formation of the Loess Plateau is pretty thick and firm. The local residents make use of the favorable landform by digging caves as residences, creating the cave dwelling architectures. The cave dwellings are troglobitic architectures. The inside of the cave is arch type, which divides the pressure of the top to the two flanks for stable gravity center and strong stability. Saying of "the cave dwellings stand erectly for hundred years" spreads among the local residents.

Some cave dwellings are excavated on the groove faces of the mountains or soil slopes. Some wealthy families combine the cave dwellings with regular houses. The rear of the residence is cave and the front is built with bungalow, surrounded by courtyard, a cave dwelling style quadrangle dwelling is completed. Some other residents excavate a square pit on the ground and dig the cave on the cliffs of the pit, which is also referred as a variety of quadrangle dwellings.

运到长安等地，史书称"万木下汾河"。然而随着地质变化和人类活动的影响，以及人口数量的不断增长，明清以来，汾河的流量已大幅减少。

渭河位于黄河腹地大"几"字形的底部，为黄河最大的支流，也是向黄河输送水和泥沙最多的支流。渭河流域范围包括陕、甘、宁三省区的87个县市，是中华民族人文初祖轩辕黄帝和神农炎帝生活的地方。尤其是著名的关中平原，大型灌区集中连片，自古以来农业发

Shaanxi, Gansu and Ningxia are scattered in the Weihe River basin, where is the living place of the Chinese nation's early ancestors the Emperor Huang and the Emperor Yan. As the famous Guanzhong Plain in the Weihe River basin has plentiful water sources, the agriculture and economy in the region have been well-developed since ancient times. The famous historical cultural sites including Yangshao culture, Erlitou culture, Qijia culture, Majiayao culture, Banpo culture and so on were all discovered in the Weihe River basin.

The Luohe River orients from the

● 流过古都洛阳的洛河（图片提供：全景正片）
Luohe River Flowing Through the Ancient Capital Luoyang

达，经济地位十分重要。著名的仰韶文化、二里头文化、齐家文化、马家窑文化、半坡文化等古文化遗址均出自渭河流域。

洛河，发源于陕西华山南麓的蓝田县，至河南省巩义市境内汇入黄河，河道长447千米。洛河流域北靠华山，地势西南高东北低，走向大致与黄河干流平行。流域内的土石山区占流域面积45.2%，主要分布在上中游地区，并有大片森林覆

Lantian County by the south foot of the Huashan Mountain in Shaanxi Province and enters into the Yellow River in Gongyi City in Henan Province. The river channel is 447 kilometers long. The Luo River basin is to the south of the Huashan Mountain. The terrain is high in the southeast and low in the northeast, generally parallels with the Yellow River. The earth-rock mountain regions area within the basin is 45.2%, mainly distributed in the upper and middle reaches areas of the river, covered with

盖，水源涵养条件较好。中游地区为黄土丘陵区，植被稀少，人烟稠密。洛河沿河河谷盆地的冲积平原是历史上文化开发较早的地区，人口密集，经济繁荣，古都洛阳就位于洛河下游盆地。据历史资料分析，洛河是黄河洪水的主要来源区之一，由于洛河邻近黄河下游，洛河发生大洪水对黄河下游威胁很大。

扎陵湖和鄂陵湖位于青藏高原巴颜喀拉山北麓，是黄河源头两个最大的高原淡水湖泊，也是黄河源头地区众水汇聚之地。两湖相距约20千米，形似蝴蝶，有"姊妹湖"之称。黄河流经星宿海和玛曲河后，首先注入扎陵湖，然后经过一条很宽的河谷，再汇入鄂陵湖。扎陵湖形如贝壳，东西长约35千米，南北宽约21.6千米，面积达526平方千米。湖水一半清澈，一半发白，有"白色长湖"之称。鄂陵湖位于扎陵湖之东，形如金钟，南北长约32.3千米，东西宽约31.6千米，湖面面积610平方千米。湖水极为清澈，呈深绿色，被称为"蓝色长湖"。

乌梁素海蒙古语意为"杨树

vast forest and abundant water sources. The loess hill regions in the middle reaches have rare vegetation and heavy population. The alluvial plain in the basin valley by the river was early developed in history, which has a tense population and prosperous economy, and is where the ancient capital Luoyang is located. According to the analysis of historical records, the Luohe River is one of the main sources of the Yellow River floods. The Luohe River is close to the lower reaches of the Yellow River, which are seriously threatened by the floods of the Luohe River.

The Gyaring Lake and the Ngoring Lake located by the north foot of the Bayan Har Mountain on the Qinghai-Xizang Plateau, are the largest two plateau freshwater lakes and the water gathering areas in the riverhead region of the Yellow River. The two lakes are about 20 kilometers in distance and look like a butterfly, so also named the Sisters Lakes. The Yellow River flows from its headstream through the Ocean of Constellation and the Maqu River to the Gyaring Lake first, then after crossing a wide valley, enters into the Ngoring Lake later. The Gyaring Lake shaped like a shell, is about 35 kilometers long

● 乌梁素海湿地景观（图片提供：FOTOE）
Landscape of the Wetland in Ulansuhai Lake

湖"，位于内蒙古巴彦淖尔，是黄河改道形成的河迹湖，中国八大淡水湖之一。南北长约36千米，东西宽约7千米，总面积293平方千米。湖上波光粼粼，白帆点点，鸟飞鱼跃，水产丰富，素有"塞上明珠"之誉。

东平湖位于山东西部的东平县境内，东连大汶河，西依京杭大运河，南临曲阜，北通黄河。宋金时这里称"梁山泊"，元明时称"鞍山湖"，清咸丰年间命名为"东平

from east to west and 21.6 kilometers wide from south to north, and the area of the lake is 526 square kilometers. The lake is half limpid half white, also called the White Long Lake. The Ngoring Lake is in the east of the Gyaring Lake, shaped like a golden bell. It's about 32.3 kilometers long from north to south and 31.6 kilometers wide from east to west, and the area is 610 square kilometers. The water is extremely limpid and dark green in color, so the lake is also named the Blue Long Lake.

The Ulansuhai Lake refering to

● 东平湖（图片提供：全景正片）
Dongping Lake

湖"。原来的东平湖是一个常年蓄水的浅水湖，湖面面积只有153平方千米。后来东平湖水库建成后，使湖面积扩展到627平方千米，蓄水量达40亿立方米，东平湖一跃成为山东省第二大淡水湖泊。

"Aspen Lake" in Mongolian, located in Bayannur in Inner Mongolia, is a furiotile lake formed by the diversion of the Yellow River and one of China's eight largest freshwater lakes. It's about 36 kilometers long from north to south and 7 kilometers wide from east to west. The total area of the lake is 233 square kilometers. The extraordinary scenery of the lake gives it the name "Pearl of the Borders".

The Dongping Lake is located in Dongping County in western Shandong Province, bordering the Dawen River in the east, the Grand Canal of China in the west, the Yellow River in the north and Qufu City in the south. The lake was named Liangshan Moor in the Song and Jin dynasties and "Anshan Lake" in the Yuan and Ming dynasties, and was renamed "Dongping Lake" in the Qing Dynasty till now. The primary Dongping Lake was a shallow lake with perennial water storage and the area was only 153 square kilometers. After the construction of the Dongping Lake Reservoir, the lake area extends to 627 square kilometers and the impoundage reaches 4 billion cubic meters, making it the second largest freshwater lake in Shandong Province.

> 黄河文明

黄河文明是世界著名的古文明之一，与长江文明并列为中国文明的两大源泉。黄河文明最初形成于公元前4000年至公元前2000年，主要集中在黄河中下游的中原地区，在新石器时代已经非常发达，具有代表性的考古学文化有仰韶文化、龙山文化、大汶口文化等，经过长时间的发展和融合，形成夏商周高度发达的青铜器文化。

黄河文明的源头

仰韶文化

仰韶文化是中国黄河中游地区重要的新石器时期文化，持续时间在公元前5000年至公元前3000年，主要分布在整个黄河中游的甘肃省到河南省之间。在已经发现的上千

> The Yellow River Civilization

The Yellow River civilization is one of the world-famous ancient civilizations and parallels with the Yangtze River civilization to be the two sources of the Chinese civilization. It first emerged from 4000 B.C. to 2000 B.C. and was mainly centralized in the Central China by the middle and lower reaches of the Yellow River. By the New Stone Age, the Yellow River civilization had been well-developed. The representative archaeological cultures include Yangshao culture, Longshan culture, Dawenkou culture and so on. After the development and merging over a long period, the Yellow River civilization grew into a highly developed bronze culture.

Source of the Yellow River Civilization

Yangshao Culture

The Yangshao culture is an important

处仰韶文化遗址中，陕西省境内分布最多，是仰韶文化的中心。

仰韶文化是以农业为主的文化类型，各氏族部落在河谷阶地上营建了或大或小的村落，过着稳定的定居生活。氏族成员主要从事农耕，饲养猪、羊等家畜，兼营狩猎、采集和捕捞鱼蚌等活动。这一时期的原始手工业也比较发达，制陶业、石器制造和其他手工业普遍得到推广和传播。其中，制陶业尤其发达，当时的人已经较好地掌握了选土、造型、装饰等工序。陶器种类有钵、盆、碗、细颈壶、小口尖底瓶、罐等。制作出的彩陶器不仅造型优美，而且表面以红彩或黑彩画出绚丽的几何图案和动物花

New Stone Age culture existed in the middle reaches areas of the Yellow River from about 5000 B.C. to 3000 B.C., mainly located within the middle reaches areas of the Yellow River from Gansu Province to Henan Province. Among the thousands of Yangshao cultural sites being discovered, most of them spread in Shaanxi Province, which is the central area of the Yangshao culture.

The Yangshao culture mainly relied on agriculture. Different tribes built vast villages in the valley and lived a steady settled life. The members of the tribes focused not only on farming and feeding livestock including pig, sheep and so on, but also hunting and fishing. The primary handicrafts of this period including pottery, stone ware

- **仰韶文化人面鱼纹彩陶盆**

  出土于仰韶文化半坡遗址，是仰韶彩陶工艺的代表作之一。盆高16.5厘米，口径39.5厘米，细泥红陶质地，内壁以黑彩绘出两组对称的人面鱼纹，象征着人们期盼富足的美好愿望。

  Painted Pottery Basin with Human Mask Motif and Fish Design

  Uncovered from the Banpo site, which is one of the representative relics of the Yangshao pottery handicraft. Made from red clay, it is 16.5 centimeters high and 39.5 centimeters across the mouth. The inner surface is decorated with a pair of human mask motif and fish design, which symbolize the wishes of wealth.

• 仰韶文化彩陶双联壶
Painted Pottery Joint Pots Dates of the Yangshao Culture

• 仰韶文化陶釜与陶灶
Pottery Boiler and Cooking Range of the Yangshao Culture

纹，其中人面形纹、鱼纹、鹿纹、蛙纹与鸟纹等形象生动逼真。

大汶口文化

大汶口文化是分布于黄河下游和江淮地区的一种原始文化，在公

manufacturing and so on were also well-developed. Among these, the pottery industry of the Yangshao culture was the most advanced. People of that time had mastered the processes including choosing soil material, shaping and decorating. The varieties of potteries include bowl, pot, cup, thin-neck bottle, sharp-bottom small-mouth pot, and jar for example. The potteries are not only beautiful in shapes, but also decorated with red or black gorgeous geometric figures and animal patterns. The patterns of human-face, fish, deer, frog and bird are very vivid.

Dawenkou Culture

The Dawenkou culture was a primary culture spreading in the lower reaches areas of the Yellow River and the Yangtze-huaihe region roughly from 4500 B.C. to 2500 B.C. Same with the other primary cultures in the Yellow River basin, the Dawenkou culture also relied on agricultural economy, and the crops were mainly the millet. The residents feed livestock including pig, dog and so on, and also engaged in fishing and hunting. The instruments of production were mainly grind stone ware including stone axe, stone shovel, and stone knife for example. The pottery

- **大汶口文化陶鬹**
陶鬹是远古时期人们用来盛酒、温酒和饮酒的器具。

Pottery *Gui* Dates of the Dawenkou Culture

The Pottery *Gui* is a kind of wine container used by the ancients.

- **大汶口文化花叶纹小口彩陶壶**

Small-mouth Chromatic Pottery Pot with Flower Leaves Design of the Dawenkou Culture

元前4500年到公元前2500年之间。大汶口文化以农业经济为主，同黄河流域其他原始文化一样，农作物以粟为主。居民饲养猪、狗等家畜，也从事渔猎和采集。生产工具主要是磨制石器，有石斧、石铲、石刀等。大汶口文化的制陶业十分发达，以三足器、圈足器和平底器较多，主要有鼎、豆、觚形杯、壶、高柄杯和鬹等。石器、玉器、骨角牙器等也很盛兴，考古发掘出

industry of the Dawenkou culture is also well-developed. The common ware shapes include three-leg ware, round-foot ware and flat-bottom ware; and the varieties include *Ding*, scoop-shape cup, pot, standing cup, *Gui* (ancient wine container) and so on. The handicrafts of stone ware, jade ware and bone artifact were also prosperous. The excavated jade broad-axe and hollow carved ivory comb for example were finely made with high craft level.

土的玉钺、透雕象牙梳等，制作精致，工艺水平很高。

龙山文化

龙山文化泛指中国黄河中下游地区新石器时代晚期的一类文化遗存，因首次发现于山东历城龙山镇（今属章丘）而得名，距今4000多年。龙山文化的经济生活以农业为主，有比较发达的畜牧业，同时占卜等巫术活动也较为盛行。从社会形态看，当时已经进入了父系社会，私有财产已经出现，这意味着阶级社会的时代已经来临。

龙山文化最具代表性的行业是制陶业，当时陶器普遍使用轮制技术，因而器形规整，器壁厚薄均

● 龙山文化陶斝
Pottery *Jia* (Wine Cup) of the Longshan Culture

Longshan Culture

The Longshan culture refers to the cultural relics in the middle and lower reaches areas of the Yellow River 4800 to 4300 years ago in the late New Age Period. The Longshan culture gets the name as it was first discovered in Longshan Town (belongs to Zhangqiu District today) in Licheng City in Shandong Province. The agriculture and stock farming of the Longshan culture were both developed, and meanwhile the witchcraft activities like divination were popular. Looking at the social formation aspect, this culture had already stepped into the patriarchal society, and the concept of private property had emerged, suggesting the arrival of the class society age.

The most representative industry of the Longshan culture is the production of pottery. As wheel tools had been commonly introduced into the pottery manufacturing, the appearance of the ware became neat and regular. The thicknesses could be well-distributed, and the quality and quantity were greatly enhanced. The pottery ware of the Longshan culture are mainly made in black pottery, which can be divided into fine silt, silt and sandy silt. Among which the fine silt is pure black and

龙山文化黑陶高柄杯
Eggshell Black Pottery Stemmed Cup of the Longshan Culture

匀，产量和质量都有很大提高。龙山文化陶器以黑陶为主，有细泥、泥质、夹砂三种，其中细泥乌黑发亮，被称为"蛋壳黑陶"，反映了当时制陶业的最高水平。黑陶以素面或磨光的为最多，纹饰较少，器形主要有碗、盆、罐、瓮、豆、单耳杯、高柄杯、鼎等。

黄河文明的发展

距今5000年前，黄河中下游地区的氏族逐渐进入了父系社会阶段，创造了灿烂的黄河早期文明。

referred to the Eggshell Black Pottery, reflecting the highest pottery making level of that time. The black potteries are commonly plain or polished, and rarely decorated with patterns. The main pottery shapes include bowl, pot, jar, urn, *Dou*, single-ear cup, stemmed cup, *Ding* and so on.

Development of the Yellow River Civilization

About 5000 years ago, the clans in the middle and lower reaches areas of the Yellow River gradually stepped into the patriarchal society stage and created the brilliant early Yellow River civilization. As the nations and cities emerged during this period and the polarization of wealth was increasingly severe for the rapidly developing of the agriculture and handicrafts, the class appeared.

By the Xia, Shang and Zhou dynasties, the Yellow River civilization enters the booming stage. On the grand plain in the middle and lower reaches areas of the Yellow River, the Heluo region culture was the core of the Yellow River civilization. The Heluo region generally contained the inner and outer intersection angles islets at the meeting point of the Yellow River and the Luohe

这一时期，邦国和城郭已经开始出现，随着农业和手工业的迅速发展，社会的贫富分化越来越严重，阶级也随之出现。

到了夏商周时期，黄河文明进入了快速发展的阶段。在黄河中下游大平原上，黄河文明的核心是河洛地区文化。河洛地区大体包括黄河与洛河交汇的内夹角洲、外夹角洲以及黄河北岸的晋南和豫北地区。在这一地区，考古发现了许多属于王朝性质的都邑遗址，包括河南登封的王城岗遗址、偃师二里头的夏文化遗址、郑州商城遗址、大名鼎鼎的安阳殷墟等，再加上西周的都城镐京和东周的都城洛邑，

River, and the south Shanxi and north Henan areas in the north bank region of the Yellow River. In this region, the archaeologists discovered many sites of the royal courts, including the Wangchenggang site in Dengfeng, Xia Dynasty cultural site in Erlitou in Yanshi, Shangcheng site in Zhengzhou and the famous Yin Dynasty ruins in Anyang for example. Together with the capital of the Western Zhou Dynasty Haojing and the capital of the Eastern Zhou Dynasty Luoyi, the capitals of the Xia, Shang and Zhou dynasties were all in the Luohe River basin, proving the Luohe River culture to be the core of the Yellow River civilization.

During the Spring and Autumn and

- **河南偃师二里头夏文化遗址出土的嵌绿松石铜牌饰**（图片提供：FOTOE）
二里头遗址位于河南偃师二里头村，是公元前21世纪至公元前16世纪的夏代都城遗址，是中国历史上最早的具有明确规划的都邑，其中已清理发掘的墓葬有数十座，其中贵族墓中随葬品非常丰富。

Kallaite Bronze Plate Accessory Discovered in the Erlitou Xia Cultural Site in Yanshi, Henan Province

The Erlitou site is located in Erlitou Village in Yanshi, Henan Province, where was the capital of the Xia Dynasty lasting from 21st century B.C. to 16th century B.C. It's also the oldest site with clear urban planning in China. Over ten tombs were found in the site, among which the tombs of the nobles were excavated with vast burial accessories.

- 殷墟妇好墓出土的跪坐玉人

妇好墓是第23代商王武丁的妻子的墓葬。据记载，妇好是一位女政治家，生前经常率军出征，开疆拓土，同时在朝中负责主持各种祭祀。妇好墓中的随葬品极为丰富，共有青铜器、玉器、宝石器、象牙器等1600多件。

Kneeling Jade Figurine Excavated from the Fuhao Tomb in the Yin Dynasty Ruins

The Fuhao Tomb is the tomb of the wife of Wuding, who was the 23rd king of the Shang Dynasty. According to the historical records, Fuhao was a stateswoman and regularly led the army expanding the territory. Meanwhile she was also responsible for the sacrifice activities in the court. The burial accessories in her tomb are extremely abundant, including over 1600 pieces of bronze ware, jade ware, gemstone ware and ivory ware.

- 河南安阳殷墟遗址

殷墟是发现于河南安阳小屯村的殷商文化遗址，从中出土了大量青铜器、甲骨文、玉器等殷商遗物。

Yin Dynasty Ruins Site in Anyang, Henan Province

The Yin Dynasty ruins is a Shang Dynasty cultural site excavated in Xiaotun Village in Anyang in Henan Province. A lot of Shang Dynasty's relics were discovered in the site including bronze ware, oracle bone inscriptions and jade ware for example.

夏、商、周三代的都邑均在河洛地区，说明河洛文化是黄河文明最核心的载体。

春秋战国时期，主要的诸侯国大都分布在黄河流域，如强大的齐国、秦国、晋国等，而楚国、吴国、越国等长江流域的国家也以向中原扩展势力为目标，黄河中下游的中原地区依然是中国主要的政治舞台。这一时期，国家机构已经发展成熟，农业、手工业、商业贸易飞速发展，青铜文化闻名中外。在文化方面，影响中国几千年的儒家、道家、墨家、法家、兵家、名家等学派也都诞生于河洛地区，它

Warring States periods, the major states were all scattered in the Yellow River basin, like the powerful Qi, Qin, Jin and so on. Meanwhile, the states in the Yangtze River basin including Chu, Wu and Yue for example were also aiming to expand their territories into the Central Plains in the middle and lower reaches areas of the Yellow River, where were still China's most important political arenas. In this period, the apparatus of states had been mature; the agriculture, handicrafts and commercial trade were rapidly developing, and the bronze culture was renowned both at home and abroad. In the cultural aspect, the influential schools of Confucianism,

- 孔子

春秋时期儒家学派的创始人孔子出生在黄河下游的鲁国陬邑（今山东曲阜）。他曾为了实现自己的政治主张而周游列国，游说诸侯。他曾经行至黄河岸边，望着滔滔奔流的河水感叹道："逝者如斯夫！不舍昼夜。"

Confucius

In the Spring and Autumn Period, Confucius, the founder of the Confucian school, was born in Zouyi (today's Qufu in Shandong Province) in the Lu State in the lower reaches area of the Yellow River. He used to travel through all the states and lobbied the kings aiming to achieve his own political view. When arriving at the bank of the Yellow River, he sighed with emotion to the torrential river, "The passage of time is just like the flow of water, goes on day and night."

们开创了"百家争鸣"的黄金时代。进入封建帝国文明的历史阶段，黄河文明达到了兴盛期。自秦汉开始直至北宋，一千多年来，河洛地区一直处于中国的核心地位。

Taoism, Mohism, Legalism, Military Strategist, Logicians and so on were all born in the Heluo region, opening the golden age of the "contention of a hundred schools of thought". After stepping into the historic stage of the feudal imperial civilization, the Yellow Civilization entered into its prosperous period. During over a thousand years from the Qin and Han dynasties to the Northern Song Dynasty, the Heluo region was sitting in the heart of China.

> 黄河两岸名城

黄河干流流经青海、四川、甘肃、宁夏、内蒙古、陕西、山西、河南、山东等9个省区，流经的重要城市主要有兰州、银川、巴彦淖尔、包头、郑州、开封、济南等。黄河靠着自己得天独厚的条件，滋养着两岸的城市，造就了这些中国名城。

银川

银川位于黄河上游地区，银川平原的中部，是宁夏回族自治区的省会。黄河蜿蜒进入宁夏境内后，一路向北流淌，由南至北纵贯银川，滋养着银川平原的千里沃野。银川平原引用黄河水进行灌溉已有两千多年的历史，农业十分发达，有"天下黄河富宁夏"之称。由于

> Major Cities by the Yellow River

The main stream of the Yellow River flows through 9 provinces and regions including Qinghai, Sichuan, Gansu, Ningxia, Inner Mongolia, Shaanxi, Shanxi, Henan and Shandong, and the major cities including Lanzhou, Yinchuan, Bayannur, Baotou, Zhengzhou, Kaifeng, Jinan and so on. With the advantageous conditions, the Yellow River created and bred these famous cities of China.

Yinchuan

Yinchuan is located in the upper reaches area of the Yellow River, the central region of the Yinchuan Plain, is the capital of the Ningxia Hui Autonomous Region. After zigzagging into Ningxia, the Yellow River heads north, cuts through Yinchuan from south to north,

历史上黄河的不断改道,银川平原湖泊湿地众多,银川又被称为"塞上湖城"。

北宋宝元元年(1038年),西北游牧民族党项人的首领李元昊在当时的兴庆府(今银川市)即皇帝位,建立了大夏国,史称"西

and breeds the vast fertile soil of the Yinchuan Plain. As the diversion irrigation history on the Yinchuan Plain is over 2000 years, the agriculture here is well-developed. For the continuous diversions of the Yellow River in the history, lakes and wetlands can be seen everywhere in the Yinchuan Plain,

● 西夏王陵(图片提供:全景正片)
西夏王陵是西夏历代帝王的陵墓,位于银川市西郊的贺兰山东麓。在方圆50千米的范围内,坐落着9座帝王陵和许多皇族和功臣的陪葬墓。这些墓的建筑形式体现了党项人特有的丧葬文化。

Western Xia Emperors' Tombs
The Western Xia Emperors' Tombs are the tombs of the emperors in the Western Xia Dynasty, located at the east foot of the Helan Mountains in the western suburbs of Yinchuan. In the area within a circumference of 50 kilometers range, stand 9 emperor's tombs and many subordinate tombs of the imperial families and meritorious statesmen. The architectural style presents the unique funeral culture of the Tangut.

● 琉璃五角花冠迦陵频伽（西夏）

迦陵频伽是一种佛教传说中能够发出奇妙乐音的神鸟，又称"妙音鸟"，是佛祖和西方净土的象征，西夏人把这种神鸟形象用于王陵建筑，喻指安葬在这里的皇帝就是西夏的佛。

Colored Glaze Quinquangular Corolline Kalavinka (Western Xia Dynasty)

Kalavinka is the bird from the Buddhist legend that can make wonderful sounds, and is also named the "Mysterious Songbird". It's the symbol of Buddha and the heavenly paradise. The people of the Western xia Dynasty brought the image of this bird to the architectures of the emperors' tomb, referring to the emperors buried as the Buddha of the Western Xia Dynasty.

夏"，将兴庆府定为首府。西夏王国共传十帝，历时190年。在此期间，中原汉族文化、北方草原文化、佛教文化等相互交融，形成了独具特色的西夏文明。银川作为西夏国首府所在地，保留有大量珍贵

giving Yinchuan the name of Lake City in North China.

In 1038 in the Northern Song Dynasty, the leader of the Tangut Li Yuanhao accomplished his succession to the throne in the Xingqing Prefecture (today's Yinchuan City) and established the Daxia Kingdom, referring to the "Western Xia" in the history. The Xingqing Prefecture was chosen as the capital. The Western Xia Dynasty had 10 emperors and lasted for 190 years. During this period, the Han culture in the Central Plain, the grassland culture in the north and the culture of Buddhism mixed together and formed the specific Western Xia civilization. Yinchuan as the capital of the Western Xia Dynasty reserves vast precious cultural relics.

As the capital city of the Ningxia Hui Autonomous Region, Yinchuan has a long history of the Hui culture, which permeates deeply into the city. Most of the Hui people believe in Islam, and have unique religious habits and living customs, like the three festivals of Hari Raya, Corban Festival and Milad-un-nabi, the songs and dances of the Hui ethnic group and the various local snacks for example.

黄河凌汛

在寒冷的冬天，黄河干流和支流的河面都会不同程度地封冻结冰。因上、下河段纬度相差较大，上段河道封冻晚、开河早，结冰较薄；下段河道封河早、开河晚，结冰较厚。每年2月下旬，气温升高，低纬度河段封冻首先解冻，水量急剧下泄，引起水位上涨；但高纬度河段因气温仍低，冰凌依然固封，在水流动力作用下，水鼓冰开，大块冰凌汹涌而下，有时冰凌在狭窄、弯曲、浅滩处大量阻塞，形成冰坝，致使水位陡涨，甚至出现冰凌漫堤的情形，形成凌灾，其危害程度常常超过普通的洪灾。20世纪中期以前，因凌汛决堤而泛滥成灾的事几乎年年发生，每次决口都给沿岸人民的生命财产带来严重的损失。

Yellow River Ice Flood

In the cold winter, the main stream and the tributaries of the Yellow River freeze in different degree. As the latitude greatly differs between the upper and lower sections, the upper section of the channel freezes late and thaws early, and the ice layer is thin; the lower section freezes early and thaws late, with the ice layer thick. In late February the air temperature increases, the section in the lower latitude region thaws first and the water rushes down causing the rising of the water level. But the section of the higher latitude is still low in temperature, and the ice is still solid. In the pressure of the flow force, the ice cracks and rapidly flows down with the water. The vast ice may blocks at the narrow, tortuous or shallow sections, forming the ice dyke and causing water to rise. Sometimes the overflows of the ice eventually form the ice floods, which commonly cause more damage than the regular floods. Before the middle 20th century, the ice floods almost happened every year and caused serious damage to the human life and property of the people living by the river.

的文化古迹。

作为宁夏回族自治区的首府，银川市的回族文化源远流长，并且渗透于这个城市的方方面面。大多数回族民众信奉伊斯兰教，宗教习惯和生活习俗都具有独特的风貌，

Lanzhou

Lanzhou is located in the upper reaches area of the Yellow River, is the capital of Gansu Province and the second largest city in western China. Near the mountain and by the river, with the Yellow River

如每年有开斋节、古尔邦节、圣纪节三大节日。回族的歌舞和各种风味小吃，尽显独特的伊斯兰风情。

兰州

兰州市位于黄河上游，是甘肃省的省会，也是中国西部第二大城

flowing through the city from west to east, the downtown of Lanzhou has a unique urban landscape. As early as 5000 years ago, human had been settled down in this place. The Western Han Dynasty set up county here and called the place Jincheng (golden city), which gradually became a major town on the Silk Road.

- 兰州黄河中山桥（图片提供：全景正片）

中山桥位于兰州市城关区，横跨于黄河之上，建于清光绪三十三年（1907年）。全部建桥材料是从德国海运到天津，再转运至兰州的。这座桥由华洋工程人员合作建造而成，是兰州最早对外开放的见证和中外技术合作的典范，有"天下黄河第一桥"之称。

Lanzhou Yellow River Zhongshan Bridge

The Zhongshan Bridge crossing the Yellow River is located in Chengguan District in Lanzhou, and was built in 1907 in the Qing Dynasty. The all building materials were shipped from Germany to Tianjin, and then transferred to Lanzhou. The bridge built by domestic and foreign engineers together, is the earliest paragon of the opening to the outside world and the Sino-foreign technical cooperation. People praised it as the First Bridge of the Yellow River.

市。市区依山傍水，黄河自西向东从市中心流过，形成了独特的城市景观。早在5000年前，人类就在这里繁衍生息。西汉时期，此地设立县治，称为"金城"，逐渐成为丝绸之路上的重镇。隋初，改置兰州总管府，始称"兰州"。随着丝绸之路的繁盛，兰州成为东西方交流的重要商埠、联系西域地区的纽带。古丝绸之路也在这里留下了众多遗迹。

今天的兰州是享有盛名的瓜果之城，白兰瓜、黄河蜜瓜、西瓜等瓜果全国知名，而且远销海内外。兰州不仅是全国最重要的铁路、公路、航空的综合交通枢纽和物流中心之一，而且是通往中亚、西亚、中东、欧洲的重要通道。

In the early Sui Dynasty, the place was renamed Lanzhou and set up with the Lanzhou Explorer House. Along with the prosperity of the Silk Road, Lanzhou became an important commercial port between East and West and the bond connecting the Western Regions. Many sites of the ancient Silk Road can be also found here.

Lanzhou is a well-known city of fruits today. Honey dew melon, melon yellow, watermelon and so on fruits are the national famous and command a ready market at home and abroad. Lanzhou is not only the comprehensive traffic hinge and logistics center of the nationwide railway, highway and aviation, but also the important passageway between East and the Middle Asia, Western Asia, Middle East and Europe.

黄河上的羊皮筏子

羊皮筏子俗称"排子"，是黄河上游青海、甘肃、宁夏一带古老的水上交通工具。用木条捆扎成方格形的木框，把一只只羊皮气囊扎在木条下面，羊皮筏就制成了。羊皮囊是将一张完整的山羊皮捆扎后充气而成。大的羊皮筏子是用6—8只皮囊并列串联而成，可载20余人；小的只用4只皮囊连成正方形，能载七八人。渡河时，乘客蹲坐在筏子中间，由三四名船工分站皮筏首尾合力划桨，将皮筏顺流驶达对岸。羊皮筏因其制作简易、成本低廉，而且自重小、吃水浅、不怕搁浅触礁、操纵灵活，在黄河上游民间得到广泛使用。

Sheepskin Rafts on the Yellow River

The sheepskin raft is commonly known as *Paizi*, which is an ancient water-transportation in Qinghai, Gansu and Ningxia in the upper reaches areas of the Yellow River. Seizing battens into square shaped wooden-frame and stabbing the sheepskin balloons below the battens, a sheepskin raft is completed. The sheepskin balloon is made in the complete sheep skin after processes of stripping, seizing and aeration. The large raft is made of 6 to 8 paratactic balloons and can carry about 20 persons; the small raft is only made in 4 balloons connecting together in square shape, and can load seven or eight persons. When crossing the river, the passenger squats in the middle of the raft, three to four boatmen stand in the head and the tail of the raft and paddle together, driving the raft to the opposite bank by the downstream. The advantages of easy making, low cost, low self weight, light-drafting, no-beaching and grounding, easy handling and so on make it widely popular in the upper reaches areas of the Yellow River.

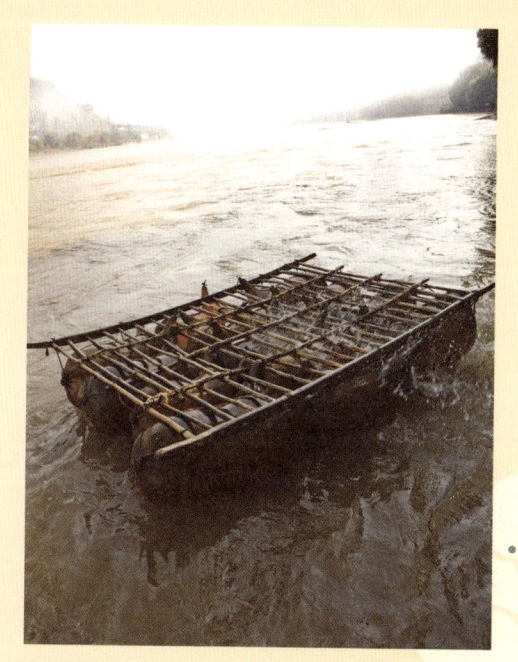

• 黄河上的羊皮筏子

（图片提供：全景正片）

Sheepskin Raft on the Yellow River

包头

　　包头是内蒙古自治区最大的城市，处于内蒙古高原的南端，北部与蒙古国接壤，南临黄河，东西分别是土默川平原和河套平原。阴山山脉横贯包头中部，形成了其北部高原、中部山地、南部平原三个地形区域。包头之名源于蒙古语"包克图"，意为"有鹿的地方"，所以包头又叫"鹿城"。这里自古以来就是多民族的聚居地，世代居住着蒙古族、汉族、回族、满族、达斡尔族、鄂伦春族等31个民族。

　　黄河流经包头的区域是原始人

Baotou

Baotou is the largest city of the Inner Mongolia Autonomous Region and is located in the south of the Inner Mongolia Plain. It is south to Mongolia, north to the Yellow River, west to the Tumochuan Plain and east to the Hetao Plain. The Yinshan Mountains crossing the central area of Baotou form the three topographic regions of the northern plateau, central mountains and southern plain in the Baotou region. The name of Baotou orients from the Mongolian word Baoketu, which means "place of deer". As a result, Baotou is also called the "Deer City". This place has been the

- 赵国的青铜钱币（战国）
  Bronze Coins of the Zhao State (Warring States Period)

● 依山而建的五当召建筑群（图片提供：FOTOE）
Wudang Temple Architectural Complex on the Hillside

类较早活动的地方，已经发掘的古人类文化遗迹有10多处。战国时期，赵国的赵武灵王于公元前306年在此筑九原城，秦统一六国后，设为九原郡。南北朝时期，北魏朝廷在包头地区设怀朔镇。元代初年，包头地区的冶炼、纺织、陶瓷等手工业开始兴盛，商业活动随之增

multiethnic habitation since ancient time, 31 ethnic groups including Mongolian, Han, Hui, Manchu, Daur, Oroqen and so on have been settled here for generations.

The Baotou region was used to be an early settle place of the hominids, and over 10 ancient human cultural remains were excavated within the region. In the Warring States Period, the King Wuling of Zhao built Jiuyuan Prefecture here in 306 B.C. After uniting the six countries, the State of Qin set up the Jiuyuan

多。随着蒙古族各部落陆续进驻河套，包头地区成为蒙汉文化交融的中心。

在蒙古地区影响最大的藏传佛教寺庙——五当召和美岱召，就坐落在包头辖区之内。五当召位于包头市西北阴山深处的五当沟，是内蒙古地区现存最大、最完整的藏式寺庙。始建于清康熙年间，后逐步扩大为今日的规模。五当召规模宏大，殿堂众多，与西藏的布达拉宫、青海塔尔寺齐名，为中国藏传

Prefecture. In the Northern and Southern dynasties, the court of the Northern Wei built Huaishuo Town in the Baotou region. In the early Yuan Dynasty, the smelting, weaving, pottery and so on industries in the Baotou region began to thrive, resulting in the increasing of the commercial activities. As the various Mongolian tribes continuously entered into the Hetao area, the Baotou region became the blending center of the Mongolian and Chinese culture.

The most influential Zang Buddhist

● 美岱召大雄宝殿（图片提供：全景正片）
Mahavira Hall in Meidaizhao

佛教的三大名寺之一。

美岱召位于包头以东，是集寺庙、王府与城池为一体的建筑群。明隆庆年间，蒙古土默特部的首领俺答汗被明朝廷册封为"顺义王"，开始建立城寺。万历三年（1575年）第一座城寺落成，寺名为"寿灵寺"。万历三十四年（1606年），西藏活佛迈达里胡图克图来到寿灵寺主持宗教活动，人们为了纪念他，将寺名改为"迈达里庙"，即"美岱召"。美岱召仿中原佛教寺庙的建筑样式，融合蒙古族和藏族风格建成，总面积约4000平方米，寺内有大量的壁画，具有很高的史料和艺术价值。

开封

开封古称"东京""汴京"，位于河南省东部，处于豫东平原的中心位置，黄河南岸，中原腹地。历史上曾有战国魏、后梁、后晋、后汉、后周、北宋、金等七个王朝建都于此，故被誉为"七朝古都"。悠久的历史，深厚的文化积淀，遍布全市的名胜古迹，使开封成为享誉全国的文化名城。

temples in the Mongolian region, the Wudang Temple and Meidaizhao, located in the Baotou region. Wudang Temple lies in the Wudang Valley in the deep Yinshan Mountains northwest to Baotou City, is the largest and most complete Zang Temple reserved in the Inner Mongolia region. The temple was first built from 1662 to 1722 in the Qing Dynasty, and gradually expanded to the scale of today. The Wudang Temple which is large in scale and has countless palaces, enjoys equal popularity with the Potala Palace in Xizang and the Kumbum Temple in Qinghai, and is one of the three major Zang Buddhist temples in China.

Meidaizhao located in the east of Baotou, is an architectural complex combining the temple, palace and city together. During from 1567 to 1572 in the Ming Dynasty, after the leader of the Mongolian Tumed Horde Altan Khan conferred the title of King Shunyi, he started to build the city temple. The first city temple was completed in 1575 and named Shouling Temple. In 1606, the Living Buddha of Xizang Maitreya Khutukhtu came to the Shouling Temple to host religious activities. In memory of him, the temple was renamed Maidali

开封地区河湖纵横,农业灌溉发达,而且气候温和,交通便利,所以成为中国开发最早的地区之一,人类活动的历史最早可追溯至

Temple, which is today's Meidaizhao. Meidaizhao combines the Buddhist architectural styles of the Central Plain, Mongolian and Zang, with total area about 4000 square meters. The vast frescos in the temple are possessed of historical and artistic value.

Kaifeng

Kaifeng was called Dongjing or Bianjing in history, located in the east of Henan Province and the central area of the Eastern Henan Plain. The city is on the south bank of the Yellow River, where is the hinterland of the Central Plain. Seven dynasties including the Wei in the Warring States Period, Later Liang, Later Jin, Later Han, Later Zhou, Northern Song and Jin chose their capitals here, which is called the "ancient capital of

- **开封开宝寺塔**

开宝寺塔位于古城开封,始建于北宋仁宗皇祐元年(1049年),是一座仿楼阁式的实心砖塔,因塔的外壁全部用深褐色琉璃面砖,远看近似铁铸,被人们俗称为"铁塔"。

Iron Pagoda in Kaifeng

The Iron Pagoda located in the ancient city Kaifeng, was firstly built in 1049 in the Northern Song Dynasty. It's a pavilion-styled solid brick tower. As the tower cliff is built in dark brown glazed bricks and looks like iron from a distance, people commonly call it the "Iron Pagoda".

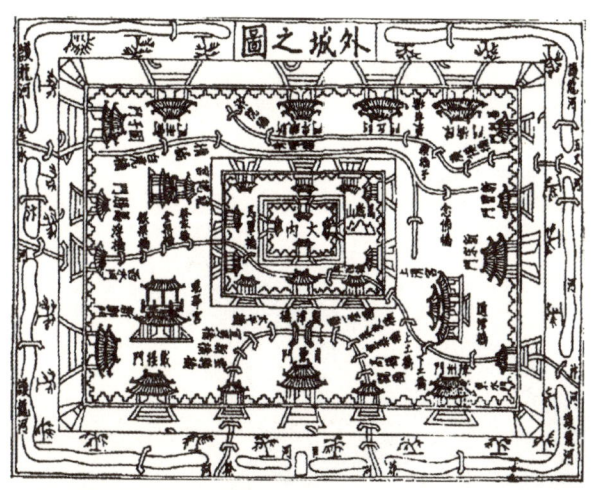

● 北宋都城汴京城市布局示意图
City Layout Schematic Diagram of the Northern Song's Capital Bianjing

seven dynasties". The long history, profound cultural heritage and scenic spots and historical sites all over the city promote Kaifeng the well-known cultural city throughout the country.

The rich water sources, developed agricultural irrigation, mild climate and convenient traffic made it one of the earliest regions being developed in China and the history of human activities in this place can be traced back to the New Stone Age. In the Spring and Autumn Period, the Duke Zhuang of Zheng State built a granary near today's Zhuxian Town in south of Kaifeng with the name of Qifeng. In the early Han Dynasty, it was renamed Kaifeng in order to avoid the name of the emperor Liu Qi. In the Warring States Period, the Wei State moved its capital to Daliang (today's Kaifeng), which was the first time of Kaifeng to be a capital. In 225 B.C., the State of Qin renamed it Junyi. In the Northern Zhou Dynasty, the Emperor Wu of Zhou chose Kaifeng as capital and renamed it Bianzhou. Since then

新石器时代。春秋时期，郑庄公在今开封城南朱仙镇附近修筑储粮的仓城，定名"启封"。汉初，为避汉景帝刘启的名讳，更名为"开封"。战国时期，魏国迁都大梁，这是开封有明确记载的第一次建都。公元前225年，秦改大梁为"浚仪"。北周时期，周武帝将其改名"汴州"，这是开封称"汴"的开始。唐代宗大历十四年（779年），节度使李勉扩建汴州城，形成今日开封城的雏形。960年，宋太祖赵匡胤建立北宋，建都"汴州"，又称"东京"。整个北宋时

- **汴绣《韩幹〈牧马图〉》**

  汴绣是中国刺绣的一个派别，起源于北宋时期的国都汴梁，当时称作"宫廷绣"，与苏绣、湘绣、粤绣、蜀绣合称为中国五大名绣。汴绣最大的特点是善于绣制古代名画、历史长卷作品，针法灵活而细腻，既忠实于原作，又表现出刺绣特有的风格。

Kaifeng Embroidery *Herdsman Painted by Han Gan*

The Kaifeng Embroidery is one of China's embroidery schools, which originates from the capital of the Northern Song Dynasty Bianjing. The Kaifeng Embroidery was called the "Palace Embroidery" in that time, and named as one of China's five famous embroideries together with the Suzhou Embroidery, Hunan Embroidery, Guangdong Embroidery and Sichuan Embroidery. The most prominent characteristic of the Kaifeng Embroidery is its suiting for the embroidering of ancient paintings and long history works. The agile and exquisite stitches not only are faithful to the original, but also present the unique characteristics of the embroidery.

期，开封繁荣兴旺，达到鼎盛，人口逾百万，成为当时全国的政治、经济、文化中心，也是世界上最繁华的大都市之一。随着城市手工业与商业的发展，城内外商业贸易十

Kaifeng is also referred to Bian. In 779 in the Tang Dynasty, the military governor Li Mian expanded Bianzhou, and the rudiment of today's Kaifeng was formed. In 960, the Emperor Taizu of Song established the Northern Song Dynasty

分发达，市民文化也繁荣发展。公元1127年，金改东京为"汴京"，是开封最后一次成为一国之都。

经过上千年的历史，开封市内遗留着众多的文物古迹，如开封铁塔、大相国寺、包公祠、禹王台等，都具有很高的历史文化价值。

and chose Bianzhou as capital, which was also called Dongjing. During the entire Northern Song Dynasty, the prosperity of Kaifeng reached its peak. With nearly a million population, it became China's political, economic and cultural center of that time, and meanwhile one of the most prosperous metropolises in the world. Along with the development of the handicrafts and commerce, the business trades inside and outside the city and the civil culture were extremely developed. In 1127, the city was renamed Bianjing by the Jin Dynasty, which was the last time of Kaifeng being a nation's capital.

After thousands years' time, numerous cultural relics are still reserved within the Kaifeng city area. The Iron Pagoda, Daxiangguo Temple, Memorial Temple of Lord Bao and Terrace to King Yu are possessed of high historical and cultural value.

清明上河图

　　北宋时期，都城汴京不仅是全国水陆交通的中心，而且商业发达，居全国之首。城中热闹的街市上开设有各种店铺，甚至出现了夜市。这一番繁华热闹的场景，被北宋时期的宫廷画家张择端画在了流传千载的风俗长卷《清明上河图》中。画面前后分为三段，首段描绘了汴京郊野的春光，点出了清明时节的特定时间和风俗。中段的主题是繁忙的汴河码头，画面上人烟稠密、粮船云集。后段展现的是热闹的市区街道，以高大的城楼为中心，两边的屋宇鳞次栉比，行人川流不息，交通工具样样俱全，反映出北宋都城商业繁荣的景象。全画场面浩大，内容丰富，画中人物多达550多个，衣着、神态各不相同，其间穿插着各种活动，富有戏剧性和韵律感。

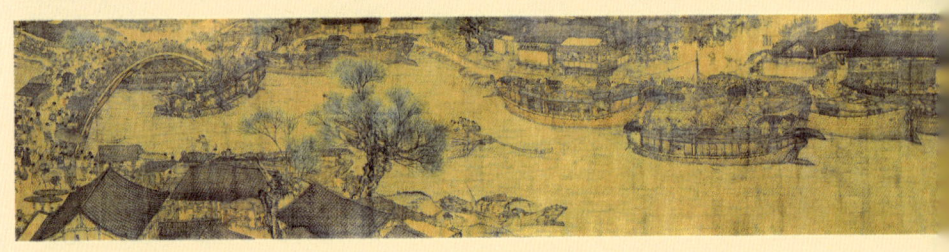

- 《清明上河图》张择端（北宋）
Scenes Along the River During the Qingming Festival by Zhang Zeduan (Northen Song Dynasty)

Scenes Along the River During the Qingming Festival

In the Northern Song Dynasty, the capital Bianjing was not only the nationwide land and water communication center, but also the business center of the nation. Various stores were opened on the busy streets and even the night market had emerged. The prosperous scenery was recorded by the court painter of the Northern Song Zhang Zeduan in his masterpiece *Scenes Along the River During the Qingming Festival*. The painting is divided into three parts. The first part describes the spring view of the suburbs of Bianjing, drawing the customs of the Qingming Festival. The theme of the middle part is the busy Bianhe River wharf, crowded with people and victualler. The rear part presents the lively streets, where high buildings, rows of dwellings, streams of people and all kinds of transportations densely scatter, reflecting the prosperous sight of the capital of the Northern Song Dynasty. The whole painting has a vast spectacle and abundant content, and the over 550 figures in the painting are totally different in dressing and expression. The various activities interspersed in the painting are theatrical and metrical.

洛阳

洛阳位于河南省西部、黄河中游南岸。古时称水之北为"阳",洛阳地处洛水之北,故称"洛阳"。洛阳地势西高东低,山陵交错,河渠密布,地形复杂,古人称"河山拱戴,形势甲于天下"。

以洛阳城为中心的河洛地区,历史上是中华民族最早的活动中心。据古代文献记载,中国最早的王朝夏、商两代就建都在洛阳附近。西周初年,都城虽然在镐京(今陕西西安),但周公为了巩固统治,在黄河以南营建雒邑,位置

Luoyang

Luoyang is located in western Henan Province by the south bank in the middle reaches of the Yellow River. In ancient times the north of a river was called *Yang*, and as Luoyang lies in the north of the Luohe River, so called Luoyang. The terrain of Luoyang is high in the west and low in the east, and with mountains crossing and rivers flowing, the topography is extremely complex. The ancient people praised it as "surrounded with mountains and rivers, the best terrain of the world".

The Heluo region based in Luoyang was the earliest activity center of the

- 周公像

周公姓姬,名旦,是西周初期杰出的政治家,西周创立者周武王的弟弟。武王死后,其子成王年幼,由周公摄政。周公先后平定叛乱,分封诸侯,营建东都,制订礼乐制度,对巩固和发展周王朝的统治起了关键性的作用,对中国历史产生了深远影响。

Portrait of Duke Zhou

The Duke Zhou named Ji Dan, was an outstanding politician in the early Western Zhou Dynasty and the younger brother of the King Wu of Zhou, who was the founder of the Western Zhou Dynasty. After the King Wu died, as his son was too young to inherit the throne, the Duke Zhou acted as regent. He squashed the revolts, created the feudal lords, built Dongdu and established the system of rites and music, which played a key role in the consolidation and development of the Western Zhou's domination and produced profound influence on Chinese history.

- 洛阳出土的三彩凤首陶壶（唐）

唐三彩是一种盛行于唐代的陶器，以黄、褐、绿为基本釉色，当时多用于殉葬，以造型生动逼真、色泽艳丽和富有生活气息而著称。

Tri-colored Glazed Phoenix-head Pottery Pot (Tang Dynasty) Excavated from Luoyang

The tri-colored glazed pottery of the Tang Dynasty is a variety of pottery being popular in the Tang Dynasty. The basic glazing colors are yellow, brown and green. The potteries were mostly used for burying with the dead, and are famous for the vivid design, gorgeous colors and the flavor of life.

就在今天的洛阳一带。西周灭亡后，周平王迁都雒邑，历史进入东周时期。到战国时期，雒邑改称"雒阳"。秦统一六国后，在河洛地区置三川郡，郡治在雒阳。西汉时期，设立以洛阳为中心的河南

Chinese nation in history. According to the historical records, the earliest royal courts of China the Xia and Shang dynasties built the capitals near Luoyang. In the early years of the Western Zhou Dynasty, though the capital was in Haojing (today's Xi'an in Shaanxi), the King Zhou built Luoyi in the south of the Yellow River in today's Luoyang region in order to consolidate the domination. After the Western Zhou perished, the King Ping of Zhou moved the capital to Luoyi and the history stepped into the Eastern Zhou Dynasty. In the Warring States Period, Luoyi was renamed Luoyang. After uniting the six nations, the Qin Dynasty established the Sanchuan Prefecture in the Heluo region and chose Luoyang as the capital. The Western Han Dynasty set up Henan Prefecture based in Luoyang, since then the word "Henan" officially became the name of the administrative division. After the establishment of the Eastern Han Dynasty, the Emperor Guangwu of Han chose Luoyang as capital and massively built palaces in Luoyang. In the late Eastern Han Dynasty, the warfare brought a big fire to Luoyang and caused serious damage. By the time of Cao Pi, the Emperor Wen of Wei, Luoyang

郡，"河南"正式成为行政区划的名称。东汉建立后，汉光武帝定都于洛阳，并在洛阳广建宫室楼台。东汉末年，各路军阀战乱不断，洛阳被火烧毁，破坏非常严重。直到魏文帝曹丕时，洛阳再次成为国都，城中宫殿才得以重建。北魏时

became the capital once again and the palaces in the city were rebuilt. In the Northern Wei Dynasty, the Emperor Xiaowen moved the capital to Luoyang, and many magnificent palaces, mansions and gardens were built within the city.

By the Sui Dynasty, the Emperor Yang of Sui changed the name of

- 洛阳白马寺 (图片提供：FOTOE)

相传在东汉永平七年（64年），汉明帝曾梦见身披金光的神人在大殿前飞行，大臣告诉他梦见的是西方的佛祖。明帝于是派人到西域求佛。三年后，使者邀请西域高僧迦叶摩腾和竺法兰，以白马驮着佛像、经卷回到洛阳。明帝下旨在洛阳城建造白马寺供他们居住。白马寺被中外佛教界誉为中华第一古刹。

White Horse Temple in Luoyang

According to legend in 64 in the Eastern Han Dynasty, the Emperor Ming dreamed of a golden immortal flying in the palace. His minister told him that the immortal in the dream is the Buddha from the west, so the Emperor Ming dispatched people to the west to pray to the Buddha. Three years later, the emissary invited the Western Regions' eminent monks Kasyapa Matanga and Dharmaratna back to Luoyang with statues of Buddha and Buddhist texts carried by the white horses. The Emperor Ming gave order to build the White Horse Temple in Luoyang for them to live. The White Horse Temple is nominated as China's first ancient temple by the Buddhist circles at home and abroad.

- **洛阳市郊的龙门石窟**

龙门石窟位于河南洛阳南部的龙门山上，始凿于北魏时期，此后的400多年间经过历代的不断建造，直到宋朝。如今有石窟1352座，佛塔40多座，另外还有题记和碑刻3600多件。

Longmen Grottoes in Suburb of Luoyang

The Longmen Grottoes located in the Longmen Mountain in the south of Luoyang in Henan Province was continuously built up in over 400 years from the Northern Wei Dynasty to the Song Dynasty. By now there have been 1352 grottoes, over 40 pagodas, and over 3600 colophons and inscriptions in the Longmen Grottoes.

期，孝文帝迁都洛阳，又在城内建起了许多华丽的宫殿、府第和苑囿。

到了隋代，隋炀帝改洛阳为东都，并且征发民夫，大举营建东都。新都建成后，隋炀帝又下令在城西兴建皇家苑囿——西苑。西苑中有人工湖、亭台楼阁、离宫别院，极尽奢靡华丽之能事。洛阳成为当时全国政治、经济、文化以及

Luoyang into Dongdu, and levied people to massively built Dongdu. After the new capital built up, the Emperor Yang gave another order to build the imperial garden the West Garden in the western city. With artificial lakes, pavilions, terraces and towers, the West Garden was extremely luxurious. Luoyang became the nationwide political, economic, cultural and the road and water transportation

河神庙嘉应观

黄河在历史上经常决口、改道，给两岸百姓带来了深重的灾难。人们除了竭力修治黄河以外，还虔诚地祈求神灵的护佑。管理黄河的神灵就是黄河龙王。黄河下游沿岸的州县都建有河神庙，嘉应观是其中最大的一座。嘉应观坐落在河南的武陟县，始建于清代雍正元年（1723年），是雍正皇帝为祭祀河神而建的宫庙合一的河神庙。据记载，建造嘉应观共耗资白银288万两，是中国历代规格最高的龙王庙。观内建筑风格与布局类似皇宫，主要包括山门、御碑亭、治河功臣殿、中大殿、禹王阁等，规模宏大，有"小故宫"之誉。观中祀奉的除了黄河龙王之外，还有历代治理黄河有功的名臣。

River Deity Temple— Jiaying Temple

The common breach and diversions of the Yellow River in history brought serious disasters to the people living by the river. Besides governing the Yellow River, people also devoutly pray

- 嘉应观御碑亭（图片提供：FOTOE）
Imperial Stele Pavilion in Jiaying Temple

for the blessing of deities. The deity governing the Yellow River is the Yellow River Loong King. The towns and cities by the lower reaches banks of the Yellow River all built the river deity temples, among which the Jiaying Temple is the largest. The Jiaying Temple is located in Wushe County in Henan Province, first built in the first year of the Yongzheng Period in the Qing Dynasty (1723). It's a palace-temple combined river deity temple built by the Emperor Yongzheng to sacrifice the river deities. According to the historical records, the construction of the Jiaying Temple cost 2.88 million Chinese taels, making it the highest-level Loong King temple in Chinese history. The architectural style and distribution of the temple are similar to the imperial palace, mainly including the Mountain Gate, Imperial Stele Pavilion, River Regulation Heroes House, Central Grand Palace, King Yu Pavilion and so on. People praise its large scale as "the small Forbidden City". Besides the Yellow River Loong King, the heroes regulating the Yellow River in the history are also enshrined.

水陆交通的中心。唐代，洛阳延续了隋朝的繁华局面，其地位与都城长安不相上下，唐高宗、武则天、唐玄宗等多位皇帝都曾久居洛阳。洛阳的商业繁荣在隋唐时期也达到顶峰，波斯和中亚一带的不少商人都在城中居住和经商。

明清两代，洛阳虽已不再是全国的政治中心，但因其独特的地理位置，依然是全国水陆交通的重要枢纽。明朝中叶，随着东南沿海地区商品经济的发展，南北方贸易也随之快速发展，进一步确立了洛阳商业重镇的地位。蒙古的皮草、新

center of that time. In the Tang Dynasty, Luoyang succeeded its prosperity from the Sui Dynasty, and equally matched with the capital Chang'an. Several emperors in the Tang Dynasty including the Emperor Gaozong, Empress Wu Zetian and Emperor Xuanzong all used to live in Luoyang. The business prosperity of Luoyang reached its peak in the Sui and Tang dynasties, and many merchants from Persia and Middle Asia were living and doing business here.

By the Ming and Qing dynasties, although Luoyang stopped being the nationwide political center, it was still the important land and water transportation

疆的玉石、山东的海盐、苏杭的刺绣、江西的瓷器、云南的茶叶等南北各地的特产都聚集在洛阳，再从这里行销四方。

作为十三朝古都，洛阳丰厚的历史文化为中华民族的发展做出了贡献，也给后人留下了无数供人凭吊的遗迹旧址。

济南

济南，是山东省的省会，黄河中下游地区的重要城市，南依泰山，北跨黄河，地势南高北低。泰山山脉丰富的地下水沿着石灰岩地层潜流至济南，被北郊的火成岩阻挡，在市区喷涌而出，形成众多泉水，济南因而素有"泉城"的美称。济南自古有七十二名泉，其中最负盛名的是趵突泉、珍珠泉、黑虎泉和五龙潭四大泉群。在市区北部，喷涌不息的泉水汇合形成大明湖，和市区南部的佛教圣地千佛山交相辉映，构成了济南"一城山色半城湖"的独特景观。

作为中华文明和齐鲁文化的重要发祥地之一，济南有着深厚的历史文化底蕴。中国上古时代的部落

hub of China for its unique geographical position. In the middle Ming Dynasty, along with the commodity economy booming in the southeast coastal areas, the trades between the north and the south were rapidly developed, further consolidating Luoyang's status of major commercial town. The nationwide special local products including the furs from Mongolia, jades from Xinjiang, sea salt from Shandong, embroideries from Suzhou and Hangzhou, potteries from Jiangxi and teas from Yunnan were all gathered in Luoyang and marketed all over the country.

As the ancient capital of thirteen dynasties, Luoyang's abundant historical culture had made a great contribution to the development of the Chinese nation, and the city reserved countless historical remains for people to visit.

Jinan

Jinan is the capital of Shandong Province and an important city in the middle and lower reaches areas of the Yellow River. North to the Mount Tai and south to the Yellow River, the terrain of Jinan is high in the south and low in the north. As the plentiful ground water of the Mount Tai flows to Jinan through the limestone

● **济南趵突泉**（图片提供：全景正片）

趵突泉位于济南市区，所谓"趵突"就是泉水跳跃奔涌之意。在长方形泉池中，三个泉眼日夜涌水不息，势如鼎沸，而且水质清净甘冽，古人常在这里一边观赏泉水，一边煮水品茗。

Spouting Spring in Jinan

The Spouting Spring is located in the downtown of Jinan. In the rectangular spring pool, pure and sweet spring water fiercely bursts from the three holes of spring day and night. The ancient people were fond of enjoying the sight of the spring while tasting tea.

联盟首领——舜就生活在今天的济南一带。传说中，舜曾在历山耕作，而历山就是现在的千佛山。春秋时期，济南地区处于齐国和鲁国的边界，成为兵家的必争之地。济南境内至今保留着修建于齐宣王年间的齐长城遗迹，西起济南市长清

formation undercurrents and stopped by the igneous rocks in the northern suburbs, the water spews out in the downtown and generates vast springs. As a result Jinan is also referred to as the "Springs City". Jinan has 72 major springs since ancient times, among which the Spouting Spring, Pearl Spring, Black Tiger Spring and Five Loongs Pool are the most famous. In northern city, the endless springs gather and form the Daming Lake, enhancing each other's beauty with the Buddhist pilgrimage Thousand-Buddha Mountain in southern city, which constitute Jinan's unique scenery of "hills and lakes all in sight".

As one of the important birthplaces of the Chinese civilization and the Shandong culture, Jinan is possessed of deep historical cultural deposits. In ancient times of China, the tribe-union

区境内，东至青岛市黄岛小珠山，蜿蜒千余里，比秦长城早400余年。秦始皇统一天下后，实行郡县制，济南地区属济北郡历下邑。汉初时设立济南郡，"济南"之名首次出现。隋唐时期，佛教兴盛，济南也留下了众多佛教胜迹，包括现存最古老的石塔四门塔，以及千佛山等地的石窟造像等。北宋时期，长时期的稳定局面使济南呈现一派太平景象，著名诗人黄庭坚曾以"济南潇洒似江南"来赞美济南的

leader King Shun lived in today's Jinan region. According to legend, Shun used to farm in Lishan Mountain, where is today's Thousand-Buddha Mountain. In the Spring and Autumn Period, the Jinan region sat in the battleground between the Qi State and Lu State. The relic Great Wall of Qi built by the King Xuan of Qi is reserved in the Jinan region till now. The Great Wall of Qi starting from Changqing District in Jinan in the west to the Xiaozhu Mountain in Huangdao in Qingdao City in the east, wriggles

● 齐长城遗址（图片提供：FOTOE）
Great Wall of Qi Historic Site

- 《李清照像》崔错（清）

  李清照是北宋与南宋之交的著名女词人，一生命运多舛，词作风格独特，将"语尽而意不尽，意尽而情不尽"的婉约风格发展到了顶峰，成为宋词婉约派代表人物之一。对后世影响极为深远。

  Portrait of Li Qingzhao by Cui Cuo (Qing Dynasty)

  Li Qingzhao is the famous female *Ci*-poem writer from the late Northern Song Dynasty to the early Southern Song Dynasty. Suffering many mishaps in her life, she achieved unique writing style of gracefulness and restraining, and developed the style to its peak. She is one of the representatives of the Song *Ci*-poems romantic school, and her influence on the later generations is very profound.

湖光山色。北宋末年到南宋时期，有两位出生在济南的文学家相继蜚声文坛，即北宋末年的女词人李清照（号易安居士）和南宋词人辛弃疾（字幼安）。他们的词作风格虽然一个婉约一个豪放，但都情真意深、语言清新，对后世词坛产

over thousand miles. It was built about 400 years earlier than the Great Wall of Qin. The system of prefectures and counties was established after the State of Qin united China, and the Jinan region was divided into Lixia County in the Northern Ji Prefecture. The Jinan Prefecture was sct up in the early Han Dynasty, when the name of "Jinan" first appeared. In the Sui and Tang dynasties, the Buddhism was prosperous and many Buddhist famous historical sites of that time are still reserved in Jinan, including the earliest stone tower reserving the Four-gate Pagoda and the Grotto Statues in the Thousand-Buddha Mountain for example. In the Northern Song Dynasty, the long-term stabilization generated the peace scene in Jinan. The famous poet Huang Tingjian used to praise the natural beauty of the lakes and mountains in Jinan "as natural and unrestrained as Jiangnan". From the late Northern Song Dynasty to the Southern Song Dynasty, two giant litterateurs were born, who are the female *Ci*-poem writer in the late Northern Song Dynasty Li Qingzhao and the *Ci*-poem writer in the Southern Song Dynasty Xin Qiji. Although one has an implicit writing style and another is bold and unconstrained, the deep feelings and

生了深远的影响，被后人合称为"二安"。明清时期，济南经济发展迅速，尤其是清康熙年间以后，济南已成为具有一定规模的商业城市。

fresh statements can be found in both of their works, which produced profound influence on the later generations. People address them the "Double *An*" together respectfully. In the Ming and Qing dynasties, especially since the Emperor Kangxi of the Qing Dynasty, the economy of Jinan was well-developed, making Jinan a commercial city in a certain scale.

黄河上的水利枢纽
Hydro-junctions on the Yellow River

三门峡水利枢纽

位于黄河上游，山西平陆与河南三门峡市交界处，1960年投入使用，被誉为"万里黄河第一坝"，是中华人民共和国成立后在黄河上兴建的第一座以防洪为主综合利用的大型水利枢纽工程。此段黄河长120千米，穿过"人门""神门""鬼门"三道险峻峡谷奔腾而来，蓄水期碧水连天，泄洪期怒涛翻卷，皆是难得一见的壮丽景观。

Sanmenxia Water Control Project

Located in the upper reaches of the Yellow River in the bordering area of Pinglu in Shanxi and Sanmenxia City in Henan, the Sanmenxia Water Control Project came into use in 1960, and is praised as the First Dyke of the Ten-thousand Miles Yellow River. It's the first large water control project built on the Yellow River for flood controlling purposes and comprehensive utilization since the founding of People's Republic of China. This section of the Yellow River is 120 kilometers long, rushing through the three hilly gorges of the Human Gate, God Gate and Ghost Gate. The scene in the storage period is like blue heaven, and angry waves can be seen in the flood discharge period which are rare sights to see.

青铜峡水利枢纽

位于黄河中游青铜峡段峡谷出口处,是以灌溉为主兼有发电、防洪、防凌等效益的大型水利枢纽工程。青铜峡枢纽工程的建成大大提高了渠道供水保证率,扩大了灌溉面积。水库波光浩渺,洲滩林草葱茏,水鸟悠游。左岸山坡上有古塔群"一百零八塔",是游览胜地,现已划为自然保护区。

Qingtongxia Water Control Project

Located in the mouth of the Qingtongxia Gorge in the middle reaches of the Yellow River, the Qingtongxia Water Control Project is a large hydro-junction. Besides the main irrigation purpose, the project can also be used for generating electricity, flood control, ice prevention and so on. The completion of the Qingtongxia Water Control Project greatly enhances the channel water supply assurance rate and expands the irrigation area. The scenery of the reservoir is spectacular. The "108 Towers" on the hillside by the left bank is a tourist attraction, and has been zoned for natural reserve.

刘家峡水电站

刘家峡水电站,位于甘肃永靖县境内,是中国首座百万千瓦级水电站。水库地处高原峡谷,景色壮观。峡谷中,奇峰对峙,千岩壁立。出峡后则高山平湖,黄土清波,水天一色。西行约50千米,就是著名的甘肃永靖炳灵寺石窟。

Liujiaxia Hydropower Station

The Liujiaxia Hydropower Station located in Yongjing County in Gansu Province, is China's first million kilowatt hydropower station. The hydropower station lies in the plateau canyon and has a grand landscape. Heading west about 50 kilometers, there stands the famous Bingling Temple Grottoes in Yongjing, Gansu.

龙羊峡水电站

龙羊峡水电站位于青海省共和县与贵德县之间的黄河干流上,是黄河上游的第一座大型梯级电站。龙羊峡水电站最大坝高178米,将黄河上游13万平方千米的年流量全部拦住。龙羊峡水电站是一座库容量为247亿立方米的大型人工水库。

Longyangxia Hydroelectric Power Station

The Longyangxia Hydroelectric Power Station is located on the main stream of the Yellow River between Gonghe County and Guide County both in Qinghai Province. It is the first large ladder-shaped power station in the upper reaches of the Yellow River. The largest dyke of the Longyangxia Hydroelectric Power Station is 178 meters high stopping the 130 thousand square kilometers' annual flow in the upper reaches of the Yellow River .The Longyangxia

Hydroelectric Power Station is a large artificial reservoir with 24.7 billion cubic meters combined capacity of storing.

小浪底水利枢纽

位于河南孟津县小浪底，在洛阳以北黄河中游最后一段峡谷的出口处，是黄河干流三门峡以下唯一能取得较大库容的控制性工程。其功能集减淤、防洪、防凌、供水、灌溉、发电等为一体，是治理开发黄河的关键性工程。

Xiaolangdi Water Control Project

Located in the Xiaolangdi in Mengjin County in Henan Province north to Luoyang and the mouth of the last valley in the middle reaches of the Yellow River, it's the only control project with a large storage capacity on the main stream of the Yellow River beside the Sanmenxia. The function of the project combines sedimentation reduction, flood control, ice prevention, irrigation and power generation together, making it the key project in the management and development of the Yellow River.

- 黄河小浪底水利枢纽泄洪的场面（图片提供：全景正片）
Flood Discharging Scenery of the Yellow River Xiaolangdi Water Control Project